Jewish Lives Project.
Public Service

First published in the United Kingdom
by the Jewish Museum London, 2017

British Library cataloguing-in-Publication Data
A catalogue record for this book is available from
the British Library

ISBN 978-1-9998246-1-7

Jewish Museum London
Raymond Burton House
Albert Street, Camden Town
London NW1 7NB
Telephone: 020 7284 7384

Jacket: the illustration of Rose Heilbron was
created especially for this book series by Laurie Rosenwald.

Cover: the cover pattern is reproduced from selected
biography images from within the book.

Published by the Jewish Museum, London, England
Designed by Webb & Webb Design Limited, London, England
Printed and bound in the U.K.

Opposite Florence Oppenheimer, page from her diary, 1918, showing a Bible that
saved a soldier's life. The top of the first page exposed reads 'Lord, who hath
delivered you out the hand of the Egyptians...', Exodus 18:10.

"Some of the officers look such boys. How many of [them] I wonder will ever come back."

Diary of Florence Oppenheimer, July 20, 1915

Acknowledgements

This book would not have been possible without the generosity and financial support of the Kirsh Charitable Foundation, and the creative vision of Lord Young. The Jewish Museum London would also like to thank the following individuals who have significantly contributed to the content of *Jewish Lives Project*. *Public Service*: Jonathan Bennett, Sacha Bennett, David Bownes, Roz Currie, Janette Dalley, Katy Ferguson, Daniel Finkelstein, Marina Fiorato, Langley Fisher, Naomi Games, Maureen Kendler, Joe Kerr, Tony Kushner, Jacqui Lewis, Ian Lillicrapp, Anna Lloyd, Rosalyn Livshin, Abigail Morris, Clare Mulley, Miriam Phelan, Kathrin Pieren, Joanne Rosenthal, Laurie Rosenwald, William Rubinstein, Sara Semic, Daniel Snowman, Rick Sopher, Morgan Wadsworth-Boyle and Brian and James Webb.

Contents

Preface

Rt Hon Lord Young of Graffham, CH.
Chairman of the Jewish Museum London

Although there were Jews living in England until the expulsion in 1290, it was only with Oliver Cromwell that they returned, in small numbers. Over many years they gradually acquired a place in society but it wasn't until the 1820s that they were admitted into universities, initially with the creation of University College London, the Godless College of Gower Street, and within a few years into Oxford and Cambridge. Admission into parliament was to take a further 30 years and happened thanks to the heroic efforts of Lord Rothschild, who stood five times before parliament relented. Although Jews were still few in number, they began to make their mark, but it wasn't until the pogroms in Russia of the 1880s led to wholesale emigration that they began to arrive in the UK in any number.

Here they found to their amazement that they had few restrictions. Indeed it could be argued that I, the elder son of an immigrant from Lithuania, was the first of my direct line to be born with no restrictions or inhibitions since the destruction of the Second Temple, a hundred generations ago. Of course there were social restrictions; for many years after the Great War Jews could not be members of some clubs, but such exclusions were made illegal and ended. Jews soon began to play a full part in the life of the nation. For many, the Great War came within a few years of their arrival, but as some of these biographies show, they conducted themselves with honour. In fact, in both World Wars, the number of Jews in the Armed Forces was well above their proportion of the nation.

They quickly learned our ways. The London Jewish Bakers Union in the early years of the last century held a series of strikes against their Jewish employers and their general secretary, Solomon Lever, an immigrant himself, was a prominent member of the TUC and mayor of Hackney. Many of the first- and second-generation immigrants were prominent in labour movements and they soon began to stand for parliament, at first for the Labour Party and in the last few decades for the Conservative Party as well.

Jews now play their part in all aspects of society, above all in public service. Prominent are those behind the great charitable foundations of our community, Wolfson, Clore, Wohl and Pears, but nameless are the literally thousands of smaller foundations and charities, individual acts of generosity, years of service in voluntary organisations helping both the wider community as well as our own.

In the closing minutes of the most solemn day in the Jewish calendar, the Day of Atonement, a prayer is said three times, "May Prayer, Penitence, and Charity avert the Evil Decree". Prayer and Penitence are self-evident but Charity, Tzedakah, is not just the giving of money, but the giving of oneself, of personal effort and even sacrifice and this is a common theme throughout this volume. These are biographies in which we can all take much pride.

Mourners gather to watch the funeral cortege of Solomon Lever, 29 July 1959

Visit the museum:
Jewish Museum London
Raymond Burton House
Albert Street, Camden Town
London NW1 7NB

Introduction

Abigail Morris
Director, Jewish Museum London

Is there life after death? That question may seem a little philosophical, abstruse or existential for a book which is very much about people and their contribution to British Society - but it is not irrelevant. The Christian concept of heaven and hell is so ingrained in our culture that it is an easy trap to fall into to imagine it is ubiquitous – that Jews also believe that you lead a good life on earth in order to secure your place in heaven. But it is not so. Sadly I do not have the power to tell you whether heaven or hell exists, but it is true that the emphasis in Judaism concerns life on earth, not the hereafter.

Jews are enjoined to become partners in the repairing of God's world. It's a daring concept: that one should have the temerity to partner with God. But whether or not Jews believe in God - and many Jews lead a very full Jewish life as either agnostics or atheists - there is no doubt that most Jews have a strong impulse to fully engage with this world for its own sake and not to earn a place in heaven. The concept is called "Tikkun Olam", which means 'to repair the world'. Jews do not believe in retreating from the hurly-burly of living, but instead see the ethical imperative of getting stuck in and trying to make a difference. Maybe the Jewish religion is less spiritual than it is practical - I'm not sure. But it is undeniably true that many Jews have a strong impulse to wrestle with the world's problems and try to make a positive difference: maybe it's their way of bringing a bit of heaven down to earth.

This energy and drive may account for many people in this book and their contribution to the life of this country. But there's another factor too.

In Judaism the word for charity is Tzedakah; however it doesn't exactly mean 'charity' – it means something more like 'justice'. Jews are commanded to give 10 percent of all they have, whether they feel like it or not; and that means all Jews, including those who receive charity themselves. All must give, even the poorest. It's quite a radical concept - to re-imagine charity as justice; to say that it is everyone's duty to make the world a fairer, more equitable society.

Another concept which is worth touching on is the hierarchy of giving. The great medieval thinker Maimonides set out and named different types of 'Tzedakah'; the number one spot is the type of charity which allows the recipient to become self-sufficient – the idea that it's better to give someone a fishing rod rather than a fish.

The Jews in this book may know about these concepts - or they may have an unconscious knowledge of them. There are as many opinions as there are types of Jews and we may not agree that their decisions and actions were invariably wise. But there is no doubt that the people in this book have wrestled with an imperfect world and tried to make a difference. We salute them.

Opposite Statue of Maimonides, Caesarea Ralli Museum, Israel

Helen Bamber OBE, psychotherapist and human rights activist.

Serving the Public: Introduction

Kathrin Pieren

Collections Manager and Curator
(Social and Military History), The Jewish Museum London

When we think of public service, governmental organisations, infrastructure and the civil service might come to mind and in fact many of the personalities in this volume were politicians, judges or people who fought in the armed forces. Yet, we want to go beyond the boundaries of state institutions and understand the term in a broader way, to include all those British Jews who contributed to the common good more generally, the people whose initiatives benefited wide sections of society, at times long after the fact. Personalities such as Helen Bamber, Nicholas Winton and the less widely known Rabbi Solomon Schonfeld worked tirelessly to help refugees, at times against political opposition, legal barriers or social narrow-mindedness.

For Jews it was an achievement to get inside governmental institutions in the first place as complete legal and social integration into British society has not always been easy. It is therefore no surprise that Jewish personalities have been prominently involved in the struggle for civil rights. The most famous example must be Lionel de Rothschild. He was elected to parliament five times before being allowed to take a seat in the House of Commons in 1858, because until then membership had required the taking of the Oath of Abjuration "upon the true faith of a Christian". Less patient but no more successful had been David Salomons, who was elected as Liberal MP for Greenwich in the 1851 by-election. He took the oath without the Christian wording and even voted in the following debate before he was made to leave the House of Commons.

That the mandatory Christian oath overruled the will of the voting population (the majority of them not Jewish) is at odds with democratic values at the service of the common good. Yet, at the time the oath was a symbol of the Christian nature of the British nation. By contributing to its abolition, these Jewish politicians opened parliament not only to their co-religionists, but to any other non-Christian faith group, making a key contribution to religious and civil equality in this country. And this was just the beginning of Jewish contributions to national politics, a broad topic that warrants its own essay in this book.

Operating outside institutions can mean doing what is not publicly acceptable, and some of the individuals celebrated in this book have not always been regarded as contributing to the common good. This was particularly the case for those who fought for the hotly contested extension of the vote to women in the early 20th century. Numerous Jewish women and men including Edith and Israel Zangwill, Henrietta Franklin and Minnie Lansbury were active members of the suffragist movement. While most did not use physical force to achieve their goals, many were subject to imprisonment and force-feeding. Today we recognise that, apart from being a basic human right, the female right to vote does not benefit only women. By participating in political life, women ensure that the viewpoints, ideas and concerns of more than half of the population are included in the public decision-making process for the benefit of all citizens.

The suffragettes had earlier role models, female pioneers who had operated on the local level where women had been enfranchised earlier or in roles for which no Christian oath was required. Yet some had other obstacles to overcome before being able to fully participate in, and contribute to, public service. An example is Henrietta Adler, whose Liberal politics met with the public disapproval of her father, Chief Rabbi and staunch Tory Hermann Adler. Unimpressed by his attitude, she went on to become a school manager, one of the first women elected to the London County Council in 1910 and an internationally acclaimed authority on juvenile delinquency. A few years later, Lily Montagu, a social worker and one of the first female Justices of the Peace, set up a movement to reform the type of religious orthodoxy her father Samuel Montagu represented. Even today she stands in the shadow of Claude Goldsmid Montefiore, with whom she co-founded the Liberal Jewish Synagogue in 1911. By standing up to their fathers and breaking into traditional male domains, both women contributed to women's emancipation within British Jewry and in British society at large.

Not only voting rights were secured for women during the transformative years of the early 20th century. In 1917, with the formation of the Women's Royal Naval Service, British women were first allowed to join the Armed Forces in non-combative roles, and in 1919 they obtained the right to work in the professions. Once they had access to these areas Jewish women participated in them just as their non-Jewish fellow-citizens did. One essay in this book is dedicated to the great number of British Jews in the legal professions, among them Rose Heilbron, only the second woman to be appointed a high court judge in the UK. Jewish women also played their part contributing to the British war effort, from Florence Oppenheimer, a nurse who served in Britain, Palestine and Egypt during the First World War, to Krystyna Skarbek, a Polish countess who, at high personal risk, put her skills into the service of the Special Operations Executive (SOE) during the Second World War. An essay dedicated to Jewish women in the SOE illustrates their outstanding bravery and commitment.

Jewish people have contributed significantly to the British armed forces at least since the mid-18th century when Alexander Schomberg renounced his Jewish faith and took the Christian sacraments, which allowed him to join the Royal Navy. Among his many military deeds was his involvement in the conquest of Quebec in the third quarter of the 18th century. Jewish men and women have fought in many other conflicts, but during the First and the Second World Wars they contributed more than the British average to the war effort. Does this disproportionate contribution mean that Jews are more publicly minded than society at large? Or could this be attributed to the (real or perceived) need to demonstrate loyalty to Britain?

Jewish men and women have made huge financial contributions not only to Jewish but also to general causes. Known philanthropists include people like Ada and Samuel Lewis, who bequeathed an enormous wealth to 51 charities in the early years of the 20th century mainly to finance housing for the working classes, and art collector Lord Joseph Duveen, who built the Duveen Gallery at the British Museum and a major extension at Tate Britain some 30 years later. Tzedakah, the religious duty to give to those less fortunate than oneself, undoubtedly accounts to some extent for financial generosity, yet, according to the essay on philanthropy in this book, not only the rich but up to 90 per cent of Jews in general give to social causes, an indicator of a disspropotionately high committment to the public good.

However, the strong eagerness to contribute to society and prove oneself in public must also be related to the fact that Jews, as a traditional social "other", have often had to combat allegations of being shirkers or profiteers. At various times in history Jewish people in this country have been made to feel that they had to make a significant contribution to the public good in order to "earn" the right of citizenship, but nowhere has this idea been expressed more poignantly than in the slogan promoted during the First World War by the *Jewish Chronicle*: "England has been all she could be to the Jews, Jews will be all they can be to England."

To finish, a few explanations regarding the selection of portraits in this book. Who is a Jew? This complicated question has been answered in many different ways across time and place. We have decided on a broad and inclusive definition. We include the children of Jewish parents – not just Jewish mothers – and each biography details, as far as possible, the person's ancestry. Being Jewish is a mix of inheritance, culture and religion. You can be an atheist Jew who practises or not. You can be born a Jew or convert to Judaism. You can be deeply religious and non-practising. It can be tribal, cultural, religious or nationalistic. In cases where people are born Jewish but disassociate, we have included them but stated that they didn't consider themselves Jewish.

Another definition we wrestled with is the question of who is British. Some on our list were born here, and some settled here. Some worked here for decades, some for a brief but significant period of their career, and it is noticeable how many of them were émigrés who found safe haven in the UK.

A book this size cannot be comprehensive, and it does not try to be, providing instead an impression of the enormous contribution that Jewish people have made to the public good in this country.

After consultations with experts, the authors carefully selected men and women from a much longer list of people who deserve to be mentioned and therefore have a profile on the Jewish Lives website. The selection for the printed book was guided by the desire to include pioneers in their fields and those whose history illustrates a particular type of contribution. Moreover, we have tried to uncover some of the less well-known stories.

For this second volume in the *Jewish Lives* series the selection was especially hard in the field of philanthropy. The most generous philanthropists tend to be wealthy business people, successful entrepreneurs. To avoid too much overlap between volumes the editorial team has decided to include some philanthropists in this book while others will be included in the forthcoming volume on commerce.

Finally, the book series only features people who are no longer with us. If you want to find out about thousands of other British Jews past and present and their contributions to British society, visit www.JewishLivesProject.com

Opposite Lord Duveen, Duveen Galleries at Tate Britian opened 1937

"When you pay high for the priceless, you're getting it cheap."
Lord Duveen

"A drunken lout of a man...
had a vote simply because
he was a male. I vowed I'd
try to change things."
Leonora Cohen

Blackguards in Bonnets! Jewish women and the fight for the vote.

'Deeds, not words', c. 1908. Imprisonment for their actions became an important tool for the Women's Social and Political Union (WSPU).

National Union of Women's Suffrage Societies (NUWSS), leaflet, 1913

Blackguards in Bonnets!
Jewish women and the fight for the vote.

Roz Currie

Curator, Islington Museum and Local History Centre

What does it mean to be a citizen in a democracy? Whether one was born in a country or came to it as a migrant, the right to vote is something that defines us and allows us to play a part in society. This essay explores the story of Jewish suffrage, and in particular the push for Jewish women for representation both within their community and in wider British society.

Jewish people had returned to Britain in the late 17th century, under Oliver Cromwell and then King Charles II. Initially their rights were curtailed as they continued to be regarded as aliens, residing in England under licence. By the early 19th century social opinion had become more liberal and sympathetic to the Jewish population. Jews were seen as an economic asset by merchants and traders, and their influence in parliament was instrumental in laws passed to put Jewish men on an equal legal footing with other men of the United Kingdom.

In 1829 British Catholics in Britain were emancipated, something both Catholic and Jewish leaders had worked towards and which gave hope for Jewish men. In 1850 David Salomons was elected as MP for Greenwich. He took his seat without taking the (Christian) oath of office and was fined by the law courts. He became mayor of London in 1855 and finally in 1858 the Jews Relief Act allowed Jewish men to serve parliament. By the end of the 19th century, various reform acts had given the vote to most men over the age of 21 and Jewish men could now practise as barristers, take a degree at university and serve openly as Jews in the armed forces.

In contrast, the position of Jewish women had seen only modest change during the 19th century. As an immigrant group, Jews were already of a lower social standing than the British majority, and women of a lower position than men. Traditional male-dominated Jewish religious practice in synagogue further reinforced women's subordinate position in the Jewish community. It was against this background that upper-class Jewish women joined others in fighting for women's rights. As parliament derided and overruled amendments to the reform acts that would give women the vote, they became increasingly active in their fight to be represented as citizens in Britain.

One of the first Jewish women to push for the vote for women was Lady Louisa Goldsmid. Her family were heavily involved in the education of women and campaigning for the rights of British Jews – including the position of women in the religion. Feeling the vote was too distant a prospect, she shifted her focus to lobbying for women in education – in 1878 London University allowed women to take degrees, and about 10 years later Cambridge University allowed women to take examinations. During the latter half of the century there were many smaller groups advocating women's suffrage. Hertha Ayrton, who attended Cambridge from 1877 but could not be awarded a degree, joined the Central Society for Women's Suffrage in 1872 while working as a scientist and inventor. The National Union of Women's Suffrage Societies (NUWSS), formed in 1897, brought together these groups under the leadership of Millicent Fawcett. They favoured peaceful protest to prove that women were responsible enough to have the vote. Dora Montefiore began her personal campaign for women when she was widowed and discovered she had no guardian rights over her children. She had been living in Australia, married to a merchant, George Barrow Montefiore, who was lost at sea. Returning to Britain, she joined the NUWSS and served on the executive committee. She became an early tax rebel, refusing to pay income tax during the Boer War (1899–1902) "a war in the making of which I had no voice", and proposed the founding of the Women's Tax Resistance League (WTRL). In 1906 she barricaded herself in her house for six weeks, refusing access to bailiffs attempting to collect tax. The "Siege of Fort Montefiore" became a cause célèbre for the nascent WTRL and Montefiore addressed crowds from her upstairs windows on the rights of women.

By the turn of the 20th century there was potentially a majority of support in parliament for women's suffrage, but the ruling Liberal Party would not allow a vote. Increasingly impatient with the lack of progress, the Women's Social and Political Union (WSPU) formed in 1903 under the leadership of Emmeline Pankhurst. The WSPU chose three colours – purple for dignity, white for purity and green for hope for the future. They held mass rallies and protest meetings, often marching to parliament and demanding their right to petition the king.

Many individuals and families from the Jewish community were active in the WSPU. Hertha Ayrton, her stepdaughter Edith Zangwill and her husband Israel joined the WSPU in 1907, helping to bankroll and support the fight for votes. Israel Zangwill shared a platform with the Pankhursts and gave rousing speeches in support of the cause. In her diary, held in the Jewish Museum collection, Edith Zangwill wrote of her young son Ayrton: "Ayrton has a way of suddenly getting on a stool and calling out 'Votes for Women' with an emphatic throwing out of his arm. A few weeks ago Israel met him coming down the middle of the village street, waving a large branch and uttering this cry. Thus, the whole family is on the propaganda tack."

WSPU Fife and Drum marching band, c.1909

Millicent Fawcett, rally in Hyde Park, c. 1915

In London, the Lowy family helped to generate support and bankroll WSPU activities. They were very involved in fundraising for the 1907 event at Princes Skating Rink, which featured the WSPU band and the sale of a specially made WSPU tea set.

Leonora Cohen from Leeds and Harrogate felt from an early age the injustice that her mother, who was a widow and head of the household, was unable to vote. In 1909, she joined the Leeds WSPU and became one of the early active members of the organisation, taking direct action to create change for women. She was very active in the WSPU ultimately becoming one of the Pankhursts' bodyguards. She said "[My husband] couldn't understand why certain women shouldn't have the vote," in contrast to one of his friends who said, "If I had a wife like yours I should tie her to a table leg."

This new movement, in contrast to that which had come before, emphasised direct action. As Israel Zangwill pointed out during a speech at Exeter Hall in 1907,

> "The agitation for Women's Rights was conducted with
> great sobriety, steadiness and moderation. And you see
> the result. Twenty fruitless years. Surely it was time to try
> insobriety, unsteadiness and immoderation."

1910 saw "Black Friday". In the face of Liberal Prime Minister Asquith's continued rejection of pro-women suffrage bills, women sent deputations to parliament. They were met with a solid line of policemen and alleged police brutality. Henrietta Lowy, her daughters and Hertha Ayrton were all members of the 1910 deputation.

Increasingly members of the WSPU took direct action against the government. Leonora Cohen and the Lowy sisters were all held in Holloway Prison on charges of criminal damage. Cohen's most famous act came after yet another meeting with parliament was cancelled. She filed down an iron bar so it would fit in her bag and smashed a case at the Tower of London that held some of the crown jewels. She was forced to the ground by alarmed Warders and arrested.

Gertrude Lowy went on hunger strike, as did many WSPU members, to protest her status as a second-division prisoner. Suffragettes on hunger strike were then force-fed, leading to a public outcry. The Prisoners (Temporary Discharge for Ill Health) Act 1913 (also known as the "Cat and Mouse Act") was a response to the outcry; it allowed the prisoners to be released on licence as soon as the hunger strike affected their health.

Another Jewish suffragette imprisoned in Holloway was Lily Delissa Joseph, an artist and sister to artist Solomon J. Solomon. Joseph was passionate in her belief in women's rights and exhibited works to support the cause. In 1912 her husband announced she could not attend the private view of her own exhibition because of her imprisonment.

The fight for women's votes split popular opinion. Women and men alike were passionately involved in the suffrage movement and found solid support in the Jewish community. "Thank God, there are Jewesses who are suffering the personal temporary physical degradation... of prison so as thereby to save thousands of women from permanent degradation and permanent constant ignominy," wrote the *Jewish Chronicle* in 1912. In contrast, others found the drive for women's suffrage unfeminine. They felt that women's "emotional" rather than logical responses posed a real danger to the future of the country. Also in 1912, the *Jewish Chronicle* reported that a WSPU window-breaker was described by the shopkeeper as a "dirty little Jewess". This exemplified the worries of the Jewish community that by sticking heads over parapets, Jewish suffragists and suffragettes were risking losing the gains in equality the Jews had made.

The Jewish League for Woman Suffrage was founded in 1912 by women from powerful Jewish families. It had twin goals; to demand that women achieved equal franchise with men and to improve the status of women in the Jewish community. It argued that there was a strong religious and moral basis to enfranchisement, particularly for Jews, who knew the evils of disenfranchisement more than most.

Henrietta Franklin, a founding member, was active in a host of liberal and feminist causes and sympathetic to her sister Lily Montagu's vision for reforming British Judaism. She formed the JLWS to rail against the educational, civic and political limits on women. Most Jewish pro-suffrage activists also donated to the JLWS. Other members included Caroline Franklin, the Zangwills and Nina Salaman, who were clear that giving women a voice could only make the Jewish community stronger.

Although the league was largely law-abiding there were more radical members. Three Jewish women disturbed a Yom Kippur service in October 1913 at the New West End Synagogue, shouting "Votes for Women," and "May God forgive Herbert Samuel and Sir Rufus Isaacs for denying freedom to women; may God forgive them for consenting to the torture of women." Interrupting worship to air grievances may be a time-honoured Jewish tradition, but such actions were viewed with horror by many in the community. They were described as "Blackguards in Bonnets!". A letter in the Jewish press read, "Dastardly crimes, of which suffragettes have been guilty... there are no lengths – or depths – to which these quasi-demented creatures will not go in their madness." (*Jewish Chronicle,* 17 October 1913.)

Many were uncomfortable with the limited scope of the WSPU and NUWSS – they felt that, by focusing on women's suffrage, it ignored the issue of emancipation for all and was absorbed with gaining votes for the wealthy. In 1913 a breakaway group from the WSPU formed the East London Federation of Suffragettes (ELF), campaigning for universal suffrage among the immigrants and poor of the East End. The JLWS opened their East End branch in the same year to engage immigrant communities and campaign for migrant rights – particularly pertinent for recent Jewish migrants to Britain, who as aliens had no right to vote and for whom naturalisation became an ever-harder goal in the face of the 1905 Immigrant Act.

Minnie Lansbury became a campaigner for suffrage while working as a schoolteacher, and joined the ELF. Lansbury was born in Stepney, east London, the daughter of Annie and Isaac Glassman, Jewish immigrants who had fled Russian persecution in Poland. She was elected as an alderman to Poplar council in 1919, while women were not permitted to serve in parliament, and imprisoned as part of the rate strikes protesting at unequal rate-setting between the boroughs.

The outbreak of the First World War split the suffrage movement again as some groups became intensely patriotic while others campaigned against the war. The WSPU suspended its activities and threw its power behind the war effort. The Women's Freedom League (WFL) and East London Federation of Suffragettes (ELF) led campaigns for equal pay, as men went to fight and women were employed in their stead, often at half the wage.

In 1918, 8.4 million women over the age of 30 were given the vote together with all men over 21. Women became nearly half of the electorate. Without the act, millions of soldiers returning from fighting for Britain would not have been able to vote. The WSPU felt that their work was done and the organisation was dissolved. Other organisations, including the NUWSS, began to shift their focus towards women's rights and equality beyond suffrage. Finally, in 1928, the voting age for women was brought in line with that for men and full adult suffrage was achieved.

Opposite Minnie Lansbury, being led off to prison, 1921

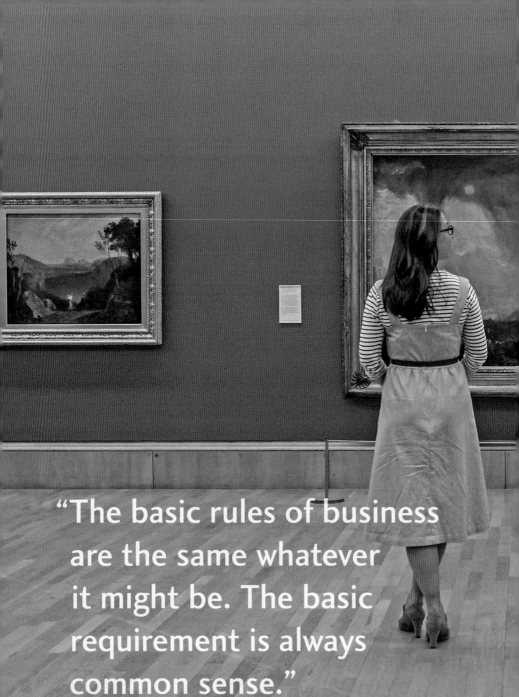

"The basic rules of business are the same whatever it might be. The basic requirement is always common sense."

Sir Charles Clore

Biographies A – D

The Clore Gallery, completed in 1987,
features work from the Turner Bequest
comprising of 300 oil paintings and many
thousands of sketches and watercolours.

Arthur Louis Aaron
Victoria Cross winner
1922–1943

Arthur Louis Aaron was born in Leeds to a Russian-Jewish father. He graduated from Leeds School of Architecture in 1941 and trained as a pilot in the USA at the British Flying School in Terrell, Texas. Aaron joined the RAF in 1942 as a bomber pilot stationed at RAF Downham Market and his first operation was a mining sortie in the Bay of Biscay. In August 1943 Aaron was flying a bombing raid over Turin, Italy, when his plane was badly damaged by gunfire. Aaron and his crew suffered injuries, and the navigator was killed. Aaron's face was injured, and he was unable to talk, so he wrote down instructions for his crew on how to land the damaged plane. Low on fuel, and at night, Aaron guided the crew into belly-landing the plane at Bone Airfield in Algeria. Nine hours later Aaron died from exhaustion, but his actions had saved his remaining crew. He was posthumously awarded the Victoria Cross for his actions, one of only three Jews to be awarded the honour in the Second World War. Recent information suggests Aaron's plane was struck by friendly fire. Aaron was proud of his Jewish heritage, but his family denied his origins following his death.

Leopold Abse
Politician
1917–2008

Leo Abse was the son of a Jewish solicitor and cinema owner in Cardiff. He was educated at the London School of Economics and became a solicitor in Cardiff, serving in the RAF during the Second World War. Stationed in Cairo, he set up a "forces parliament" but was arrested, and the so-called "parliament" dissolved, when he moved a motion calling for the nationalisation of the Bank of England. Abse was elected to the House of Commons as a Labour MP at a by-election in 1958, serving until 1987. There, he became known as a campaigner to liberalise the laws on divorce and homosexuality. On other issues, such as abortion, Abse was, however, a conservative. He was also known for, bizarrely, dressing with flamboyant eccentricity on Budget Day, and for writing "psycho-biographies" of Margaret Thatcher and Tony Blair. He was a strong supporter of Israel and of Poale Zion. His brother, Dannie Abse (1923–2014), was a distinguished poet.

Desmond Ackner
Judge and Lord of Appeal
1920–2006

Desmond Ackner was born in Islington, London, the son of an immigrant Viennese dentist and an English-Jewish mother, Rhoda née Tuck. He was educated at Highgate School and Clare College, Cambridge. He became a barrister in 1945 and Queen's Counsel in 1961. He represented the victims of the drug Thalidomide and the families of the Aberfan coal tip disaster (1966). He became Judge of the Appeals Court of Jersey and Guernsey and Chairman of the Bar Council. In 1971 he was appointed a high court judge and received a knighthood. He went on to be a judge of the commercial court and of the western circuit. In 1980 he became a lord justice of appeal, a privy counsellor and President of the Senate of the Inns of Court. In 1986 he was created Baron Ackner of Sutton and a lord of appeal in ordinary. He was one of the three law lords who blocked publication of the book *Spycatcher.* In 1946 he married Joan Spence and had three children. While Ackner was raised as a Jew, his children were baptised and confirmed as Anglicans. He loved the open air and sailed his own yacht, gardened and swam in his pool whatever the weather.

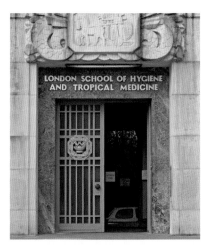

LONDON SCHOOL OF HYGIENE AND TROPICAL MEDICINE

Abraham Manie Adelstein
Chief Medical Statistician at the OPCS
1916 – 1992

Abraham Manie Adelstein, known simply as "Abe", was born in South Africa to Nathan Adelstein and Rosie Cohen, Jewish immigrants from Latvia. After studying medicine at Witwatersrand University and doing military service in the South African Medical Corps, he was appointed Health Officer at the South African Railways. In 1951, Adelstein came to the London School of Hygiene and Tropical Medicine to study medical statistics. He returned to South Africa in 1953 to become Director of Research and Medical Statistics for the South African Railways. Growing increasingly frustrated with the political situation there, he left in 1961 to become a senior lecturer in social and preventive medicine at Manchester University. In 1967, he joined the General Register Office (later OPCS) as Chief Medical Statistician, where he helped to improve the national cancer registration scheme and was frequently consulted over the wide range of surveys related to health matters. Adelstein's interests in social medicine led him to play a leading part at meetings of the World Health Organization and in the development of recommendations for health information systems across Europe. After retiring in 1981, he continued his research interests as Visiting Professor of Epidemiology at the London School of Hygiene and Tropical Medicine, a post he held until 1984.

Henrietta Adler

Groundbreaking politician
elected to the London
County Council
1868–1950

Henrietta Adler was born in
London and was the daughter
of Rabbi Dr Hermann Adler.
She became a school manager
under the London School Board.
Adler's political career was inspired by a heartfelt desire to improve
the living conditions of London's poor, particularly the inhabitants
of the slums in the East End. She was a member of the Progressive
Party and in 1905 joined the education committee of the London
County Council (LCC). She was elected to the LCC in 1910, rising to
Deputy Chairman in 1922. After the Liberal government overturned
legislation excluding women from LCC membership, they put Adler
forward as the candidate for the Central Hackney division. She won
the election comfortably, becoming one of the first women to sit on
the council, and used her position to bring more attention to the
issue of child poverty. Adler remained faithful to her Orthodox Jewish
heritage, refusing to campaign on Saturdays during the LCC elections.
Adler was awarded the OBE in 1934.

Edward Ephraim Alex

Founder of the Jewish Board
of Guardians
1800–1882

Edward Ephraim Alex, born in
the City of London, was the
eldest surviving son of dentist
Solomon Alex and his wife Rachel.
He married a widow, Catherine,
in 1840 and practised as a
dental surgeon in Blackfriars and later in Westminster. A charitable
system for poor Jews of German and Polish descent had been
established in 1753 to look after a community of 8,000 but this
number had increased to 40,000 by 1858. Abraham Benisch of the
Jewish Chronicle put forward an idea that the three City synagogues
form a board of guardians and Alex, who was overseer of the Great
Synagogue, made a modified proposal that the existing board be
expanded and given an independent staff to deal with the foreign
poor. The severe winter of 1858–1859 necessitated this proposal
to be implemented urgently and finally, on 16 March 1859, the first
meeting of the Board of Guardians was held at the Great Synagogue.
Alex was elected as president, remaining so for 10 years, only retiring
due to ill-health. The Jewish Board of Guardians merged with Jewish
Blind Society to become what is known as Jewish Care today.

Hanns Alexander
Nazi hunter
1917–2006

Hanns Alexander was born in Berlin to Alfred and Henny Alexander, 15 minutes before his twin, Paul. In 1933, following Hitler's rise to power, Alexander and his family were forced to leave their home due to persecution. Alexander moved to London in 1936. After the Second World War ended and the true horror of the death camps was revealed, Alexander was deeply affected by the realisation that the Germans with whom he had grown up had committed such atrocities. He channelled his rage into finding Nazis to bring to trial. Using his native German, Alexander was able to translate and transcribe the affidavits of some of the key players in the execution of the Holocaust. He captured the Kommandant of Auschwitz, Rudolf Höss, whose confession and information regarding the implementation of the Final Solution led to a new understanding of what happened in the camps and also encouraged other Nazis to confess at various trials. In his later years Alexander became a merchant banker with S.G. Warburg in the City of London. He always remembered his Jewish roots and became active in the running of the Belsize Square Synagogue. He donated the Alexander family Torah, commissioned in 1790, to the synagogue, where it is still used to this day.

Leopold Charles Maurice Stennett Amery

Politician and author of the
Balfour Declaration
1873–1955

L.S. Amery was born in India, the
son of Charles Frederick Amery,
a non-Jewish official in the
Indian Forestry Commission, and
Elisabeth Sapir (or Saphir), born
in Budapest to a distinguished Jewish family. Amery concealed his
Jewish background throughout his life, changing his original middle
name of "Moritz" to "Maurice." Educated on a scholarship at Harrow
School, and then at Balliol College, Oxford, he became a Fellow
of All Souls. A lifelong advocate of Joseph Chamberlain's proposal
for Imperial Preference, he supported the placing of a tariff barrier
around the whole British Empire, ending Britain's policy of free trade.
Amery was elected to parliament in 1911, serving until 1945. In 1917
as a junior minister he was given the task of drafting the Balfour
Declaration, the wording of which is essentially Amery's. From 1924–
29 he served as Secretary of State for the Dominions and Colonies,
and facilitated the development of the infrastructure of Palestine.
In 1940 he was a major participant, against the Chamberlain
government, in the famous debate that brought Winston Churchill
to power as Prime Minister. The great tragedy of Amery's life was
that his eldest son, John Amery (1912–45), became an enthusiastic
Nazi, broadcasting on German radio in favour of the Axis, despite
his Jewish ancestry. In 1945 John Amery was convicted of treason
and hanged.

Vera Atkins
Spymaster
1908–2000

Vera Maria Rosenberg was born in Bucharest, Romania, to German-Jewish father, Max, a timber merchant, and British-Jewish mother, Zeffro Hilda, née Atkins. The family moved to England in 1933. Atkins studied modern languages at the Sorbonne and attended finishing school at Lausanne, becoming fluent in French. In 1941 Atkins was recruited into the Special Operations Executive and assigned to F-Section, where she was given the responsibility of recruiting women agents in France. Part of her role included sending clandestine messages from the agents via the BBC to their next of kin. This loyalty for those in her charge continued after the war, when Atkins worked for the British War Crimes Commission, gathering evidence to assist in the prosecution of war criminals, including the Kommandant of Auschwitz, Rudolf Höss. Höss was coerced into admitting he had overseen the deaths of 960,000 Jews. Atkins also sought out the fates of 118 missing agents. Only one eluded her, an agent who had been given three million francs for operations, but gambled it in a Marseille casino before disappearing. In 1987, Atkins was awarded the *Légion d'honneur*, and a British CBE in 1997. She was the cousin of Rodolf Vrba, who co-authored the Vrba-Wetzler Report detailing the scale and nature of the massacre at Auschwitz.

Hertha Ayrton

Scientist, inventor and suffragist
1854–1923

Hertha Ayrton was born Phoebe Sarah Marks in Portsea, Hampshire. Her watchmaker father, Levi Marks, was a Polish immigrant who came to England to escape the pogroms. Her mother, Alice Moss, was a Jewish seamstress from Portsea. Ayrton and her family were proud of their Jewish heritage, though most were agnostic. Ayrton read mathematics at Girton College, Cambridge from 1877. Her mentor, Barbara Bodichon, was a women's activist and co-founder of Girton. In 1872, Ayrton joined the Central Society for Women's Suffrage. In 1907 she joined the Women's Social and Political Union (WSPU), which was the militant wing of the women's suffrage movement, helping to finance the organisation. She was part of the Black Friday deputation to parliament in 1910, which was met with alleged police brutality. Ayrton was a founder member of the Jewish League for Woman Suffrage and joined the United Suffragists in 1914, after deciding that the WSPU's tactics had become ineffective. She was an important figure in mathematics and engineering. Following work on ripples in sand and water, she developed an anti-gas fan to use in the trenches during the First World War, which she lobbied to be deployed. Eventually over 100,000 came into use.

John Balcombe
Lord Justice of Appeal
1925–2000

John Balcombe was born in Willesden, London. His father was the proprietor of Alba, which manufactured radios and TVs. He was educated at Winchester College and New College, Oxford. He became a barrister in 1950 and built up a large practice. He was appointed Queen's Counsel in 1969, a high court judge of the family division from 1977 and was knighted in the same year. In 1985 he was promoted to the court of appeal and became a member of the privy council. He served on the court of appeal until 1995. In one legal case Balcombe saved the famous Aintree racecourse from development. He was well-respected for his sound judgement and brilliant mind. Outside the legal profession, he was an active Mason and chairman of the Marriage Guidance Council and participated in the Jewish community. He was president of the Maccabaeans, a Jewish cultural society, chairman of the Friends of the Hebrew University legal group and trustee of the Wimbledon and District Reform Synagogue. He supported Norwood, the Jewish orphanage, and Nightingale House, a Jewish care home. John's religion did not prevent him becoming Dean of Chapel of Lincoln's Inn in 1955. This administrative office required attendance at the Anglican chapel services, where he regularly read the Old Testament lesson.

Helen Bamber

Dedicated her life to supporting
victims of torture
1925–2014

Helen Bamber was born Helen
Balmuth in Stamford Hill, north
London, to Jewish parents. Her
father Louis Balmuth, whose
family originated in Poland,
taught her about the threat of
Nazism by reading passages of *Mein Kampf* to her. Aged 20, Bamber
volunteered to work with survivors of the Holocaust in the recently
liberated concentration camp of Bergen-Belsen in Germany, where
she stayed for two years. On her return to Britain, she trained to
work with disturbed young adults and children and took a degree in
social science at the London School of Economics. In 1947, Bamber
was appointed to the Committee for the Care of Children from
Concentration Camps. In 1961, Bamber joined Amnesty International
where she provided therapy to victims of trauma. After many years
working for Amnesty, Bamber established the Medical Foundation for
the Care of Victims of Torture in 1985, which treated up to 3,000
patients a year from almost 100 countries. In 2005, she founded the
Helen Bamber Foundation, to expand her work with torture survivors
to include those suffering other forms of human rights violations.
Bamber was named European Woman of Achievement in 1993 and
was awarded the OBE in 1997 in recognition of her work.

Joel Barnett
Politician
1923–2014

Joel Barnett was born in Manchester, the son of Louis and Ettie Barnett. His father was a tailor, and the family lived in poverty. Barnett, was educated at Badkindt Hebrew School and Manchester Central High School, and served during the Second World War in the Royal Army Service Corps. A trained accountant, he was a member of the Prestwich Borough Council from 1956–59, and served as a Labour MP from 1964 until 1983, when he was awarded a life peerage as Baron Barnett. He served as Chief Secretary to the Treasury from 1974 to 1979, and was a member of the Cabinet from 1977 to 1979. He was a major advisor to Denis Healey, Chancellor of the Exchequer, and also served as Chairman of the Commons' Public Accounts Committee from 1979–83. He is best known for having devised the "Barnett Formula" for apportioning government money to England, Scotland, Wales and Northern Ireland. Barnett served as Vice-Chairman of the board of governors of the BBC from 1986–93, and wrote an autobiography, *Inside the Treasury* (1982).

Leslie Hore-Belisha

Politician who introduced
Belisha Beacons

1893–1957

Leslie Hore-Belisha was born in London. His father, a Sephardi Jew, died when Leslie was young. Belisha laid the groundwork for his political career at St John's College, Oxford; he was elected President of the Oxford Union in 1919 after returning from service with the Royal Fusiliers in France. Belisha became the Liberal MP for Plymouth Devonport in 1923. He was given the transport portfolio in 1934 and supported a number of safety provisions including the driving test, a new highway code and his namesake the Belisha beacons. Aged only 43, Belisha became the Secretary of State for War with a mandate to revitalise the War Office. He tried to avoid committing British forces to a continental conflict, but his antipathy towards Germany strengthened after the Munich Crisis, opposing Appeasement and advocating military action instead. Belisha fell foul of the military leadership during the war and was removed from his post. He turned down the presidency of the Board of Trade and was allegedly not offered the role of Minister of Information because he was Jewish. He did, however, serve briefly as Minister of National Insurance in Churchill's caretaker government in 1945, and was created Baron Hore-Belisha in 1954.

Judah Philip Benjamin
Confederate senator and
Queen's Counsel
1811 – 1884

Judah Benjamin was born in
the British island of St Croix
in the West Indies. His parents
were Sephardi Jews who had
left Britain in 1807. He grew up
in Fayetteville, North Carolina
and was educated at a local school and then at Yale College. He
became a barrister in 1832. In 1848 he was admitted as Counsellor of
the Supreme Court. He was also involved in politics and was elected
senator for Louisiana in 1852. He participated in the temporary
government of the Southern Confederacy in 1861, first as Attorney
General, then as Secretary of War and Secretary of State. On the fall
of the Confederacy Judah fled to Britain in 1865. He enrolled as a law
student at Lincoln's Inn and became a barrister in 1866, joining the
northern circuit. In 1868 he published a book on the contract of sale,
which became a standard legal text. In 1872 he received a patent
of precedent that allowed him the privileges of a member of the
Queen's Counsel. Benjamin was brought up in an observant Jewish
family, but, he married a Roman Catholic Creole and did not identify
himself with the Jewish religion.

Inez Bensusan

Helped found the Actresses'
Franchise League
1871 – 1967

Inez Bensusan was born into
a wealthy Jewish family in
Sydney, Australia. Her father
was Samuel Levy Bensusan, a
mining agent. After settling in
Britain in the 1890s, Bensusan
worked as an actress and became an active campaigner for women's
suffrage. She joined the Women's Social and Political Union in 1908
and was a founding member of the Actresses' Franchise League
(AFL), which performed pro-suffrage plays. Bensusan wrote several
plays herself, including *The Apple* and *Nobody's Sweetheart*. She also
wrote, produced and starred in the film *True Womanhood* in 1911. The
demand for suffrage plays led the AFL to set up a play department,
which was run by Bensusan, who was able to persuade both men and
women to write for it. This widened the audience as the male voice
had more authority in Edwardian England. Bensusan was an executive
member of the Jewish League for Woman Suffrage. Both men and
women were encouraged to join and subscriptions were set at a level
that allowed people from all classes to become members. Although
the league's work focused mainly on the issue of suffrage, it also
strove to improve the conditions of women in the Jewish community.

Herbert Bentwich

Lawyer, communal worker
and Zionist
1856–1932

Herbert Bentwich was born in Whitechapel, London. His father was an immigrant from Russian Poland. He grew up in Bishopsgate in the City of London. Herbert was educated at Woodman's School, Bishopsgate, a Jewish boarding school in Edmonton, the Whitechapel Foundation and University College London. He became a solicitor specialising in copyright law and was appointed to the London Chamber of Arbitration. In 1903 he became a barrister for the south-eastern circuit but gave it up to acquire and edit the *Law Journal*. Herbert was active and held office in many Jewish communal organisations including the Board of Deputies, the Jewish Board of Guardians, the Stepney Jewish schools, the education committee of Jews' College, St John's Wood Synagogue and the Chevra Kadisha burial society. He was a founder of the first lodge of England's Independent Order of Bnai Brith, Hampstead Synagogue and the Society of Jewish Jurisprudence. Herbert was one of the pioneers of Zionism in England. He was a founder of the British Zionist Federation in 1899 and its Vice-Chairman, and was Legal Advisor for the Jewish Colonial Trust. He was a leading member of the Chovevei Zion movement, Foundation Chairman of the English Zionist Federation, a member of the Presidential Council of Zionist Congresses and Grand Commander of the Zionist friendly society the Order of Ancient Maccabeans. He had nine daughters and two sons, and eventually settled in Jerusalem in 1929.

Norman Bentwich

Barrister, academic and Zionist
1883–1971

Norman Bentwich was born in London to Herbert Bentwich, whose father had been an immigrant from Russian Poland. He was educated at St Paul's School and Trinity College, Cambridge. He became a barrister and in 1912 worked for the Ministry of Justice in Cairo. In 1915 he joined the British army in Egypt and rose to the rank of lieutenant colonel. He was awarded the Military Cross and OBE. Herbert became Legal Secretary to the British military administration and in 1922 the first Attorney General to the British Mandate in Palestine. Despite working for Arab–Jewish understanding, he was removed to placate Arab opinion, retiring from the colonial service in 1931. He became Professor of International Relations at the Hebrew University of Jerusalem and worked with the League of Nations and the Council for German Jewry to rescue refugees from Nazism. During the Second World War Herbert served in the Ministry of Information in London, and was Chairman of the National Peace Council, a coordinating organisation for almost 200 peace groups around Britain. Bentwich played an important role in the development of modern commercial law in Palestine. He was a professor at the Hebrew University from 1932–51. After retirement, he joined the Hebrew University board of governors. Bentwich then settled in Britain and served as President of the North-Western Reform Synagogue in London from 1958 and authored nearly 30 books.

Gilbert Beyfus

Barrister who represented
Aneurin Bevan
1885–1960

Gilbert Beyfus was born in
Kensington, London, the only
son of Alfred Beyfus, a solicitor
of Germanic Jewish origin, and
his wife, Emmie Ruth Plumstead.
Beyfus was educated at Harrow
School and Trinity College, Oxford, where he switched from history
to jurisprudence in 1907. In 1908, he was called to the bar in the
Inner Temple. On the outbreak of the First World War, Beyfus was
commissioned as a second lieutenant. Taken captive in 1915, he
remained a prisoner of war until 1918. A year later, he retired as a
captain and returned to his career at the bar. Beyfus also tried his
hand at politics, standing as Liberal candidate for Cirencester in
1910 and as coalition candidate for Kingswinford in 1922. However,
his political ambitions were dashed after he was rejected on both
occasions. In 1933, Beyfus became Queen's Counsel and in 1940 was
made Bencher of his inn. He appeared in many of the great trials of
his times, representing Aneurin Bevan, Richard Crossman and Morgan
Phillips (chairman of the Labour Party) in their "Venetian Blind"
action against the *Spectator* in 1957, when the magazine suggested
the three had been drinking heavily on a trip to Venice. It transpired
later that the trio were guilty. Beyfus retired from the bar in 1960,
after being diagnosed with terminal cancer. He was a lavish host, who
loved the theatre as well as hunting, fishing and tennis.

Hannah Billig

"The Angel of Cable Street"

1901 – 1987

Hannah Billig was born in London's East End to father Barnet, a newsagent, and mother Millie. Both were Orthodox Jews who had escaped the pogroms in Russia. In 1912 Billig won a scholarship to Myrdle Road Central School and then a scholarship to London University to study medicine. In 1925, Billig qualified as a doctor at the Royal Free Hospital and later joined the Jewish Maternity Hospital in Underwood Street. In 1927, Billig opened her own surgery at Watney Street, Shadwell. Pre-NHS, Billig treated patients whether they could pay or not. During the Second World War, she volunteered to provide medical assistance to air raid shelterers in Wapping. In 1941, while tending those injured in a raid at Orient Wharf, Billig had her ankle broken by a bomb blast, but continued treating the wounded and was awarded the George Medal for her bravery. Locals in the area began calling her "The Angel of Cable Street", after the street where her new surgery was situated. In 1942, Billig joined the Indian Army Medical Corps as a captain, serving in Assam, tending soldiers from the Burma conflict. She was awarded the MBE in 1945. She retired to Israel in 1964.

Alma Birk
Journalist and politician
1917–1996

Alma Birk was born in Brighton. She was the daughter of Barnett Wilson (né Woolfson), founder of Wilson Brothers Greeting Cards Ltd., and Alice Tosh. Educated at South Hampstead High School and the London School of Economics, Birk was elected Labour member of the Finchley Borough Council, a position she held from 1950–1953. She stood for parliament on three occasions, losing each time. Birk was an accomplished journalist, beginning her career with a column in Labour weekly Forward, from which she moved to the Daily Herald. A stint as Associate Editor of women's magazine Nova followed from 1965–1969. A daring publication looking frankly at social and sexual problems, the magazine was a forerunner of more successful rival Cosmopolitan, which forced Nova out of business. When Nova folded Birk turned her full attention back to politics. In 1967 Harold Wilson recognized Birk's political activities with a life peerage (as Baroness Birk). In the House of Lords, she served in a number of posts in the Labour government, including that of Parliamentary Undersecretary for the Environment from 1974–79. She was a member of the Executive of the Council of Christians and Jews and served on the Holocaust Memorial Committee. Her husband Ellis Birk served as editorial director of the *Sunday Pictorial* and the *Mirror* newspaper group, as chairman of the *Jewish Chronicle* newspaper, and as chairman of the Jewish Welfare Board.

Denise Bloch
SOE agent
1916–1945

Denise Bloch was born in born in Paris. Her family hid from the Nazis before moving to Lyon in 1942, just managing to evade the mass deportation of Jews. She joined the Resistance and became part of an SOE network, working with radio operator John Stonehouse. After he and others in the network were arrested she went into hiding. Bloch escaped to Spain by walking over the Pyrenees and arrived in London in May 1943. The SOE were reluctant to send her back to France as she was known to the Gestapo, but she was eventually trained as a wireless operator and in March 1944 was landed in France with former racing driver Robert Benoist to mobilise resistance in the Nantes area. She was captured with her group in June and taken to Paris, where she was interrogated. In August she was transferred to Ravensbrück concentration camp along with SOE agents Violette Szabo and Lilian Rolfe. After hard physical labour at various camps during the winter their health deteriorated, and in January 1945 they were all executed at Ravensbrück. Bloch was posthumously awarded the King's Commendation for Brave Conduct, the Croix de Guerre, the Légion d'honneur and the Médaille de la Résistance and is commemorated at various SOE memorials.

Edward Brampton

Godson of King Edward IV, knight
and military commander
1440–1508

Edward Brampton was born
Duarte Brandão in Portugal,
the son of a Jewish mother. He
emigrated to England, entered
the House of Converts and
converted to Christianity in
1468. As was the convention on conversion, King Edward IV became
his nominal godfather. Edward became a soldier for the king and in
1472–73 he jointly commanded an armed force at sea during the
Wars of the Roses. He was made a naturalised citizen and granted
property in London for his services. In 1475 he accompanied the
invasion of France and was rewarded by the king and the Duke
of Burgundy with a grant of arms. In Bruges he began to build
up trading interests between England, southern Iberia and the
Low Countries and he became Master of the Drapers' Company
of London from 1477–78. As a reward for financially helping the
Portuguese King Alfonso V return to Portugal, he was renaturalised
as a Portuguese citizen in 1479 and given property and trading
privileges. In England in 1482 he was appointed Governor of
Guernsey and a courtier of the king and in 1484 he was knighted by
Richard III. With Richard's defeat at the battle of Bosworth (1485),
Edward lost his governorship and his properties and left for Lisbon,
where he died.

Leon Brittan

Conservative MP and minister
1939–2015

Leon Brittan was born in London to parents of Lithuanian origin. His father was a doctor who had arrived in England as a refugee in the late 1920s. The family was Orthodox and Leon remained committed to his Jewish heritage. Brittan studied at Trinity College, Cambridge, where he was President of the Union, and was called to the bar in 1962. His parliamentary career began in 1974 when he was elected Conservative MP for Cleveland and Whitby. Due to boundary changes, he was re-elected as MP for Richmond, Yorkshire in 1979. Under Margaret Thatcher, Brittan served as Chief Secretary to the Treasury. In 1983 he was appointed Home Secretary. In this post, Brittan attempted to streamline the bureaucracy of the Home Office. He also introduced tougher prison sentences for offenders. In 1986 he resigned over the Westland Crisis when it emerged he had authorised the leak of a letter that criticised the Defence Secretary Michael Heseltine. In 1989 Brittan moved to Brussels, working as a European commissioner. He promoted free trade across Europe and was appointed a Vice-President of the European Commission in 1993. Brittan published two works on the United Kingdom's relationship with Europe, *The Europe We Need* (1994) and *A Diet of Brussels* (2000). Brittan was knighted in 1989 and made a life peer in 2000. Sir Samuel Brittan of the *Financial Times* is his brother.

John Burgh

Civil Servant

1925–2013

John Charles Burgh was born in Vienna to Jewish parents. His barrister father died of leukaemia when Burgh was 12 but had converted to Catholicism and sent Burgh to a Catholic school. Fleeing the Nazis in 1938, Burgh arrived in England unable to speak the language, but at the British embassy he was taught the Lord's Prayer and baptised. Burgh was initially reluctant to discuss his Jewish heritage but over time embraced it. In 1946 Burgh attended night classes at the London School of Economics, winning a bursary to study full-time. He was elected President of the Student Union in 1949 and he was a co-founder of The Seminar group there. Burgh joined the civil service, working for many departments including in a position underneath Lord Rothschild. Burgh was appointed Head of the British Council in 1980 and turned the failing institution into a successful organisation over his seven-year tenure. He was was knighted in 1982, and in 1987 he was chosen to be president of Trinity College, Oxford where he remianed until his retirement in 1996.

Gerald Butler
Judge
1930–2010

Gerald Butler was born in Hackney, east London, and grew up in Ilford. His maternal grandfather had emigrated from Austria. He was educated at Ilford County High School, the London School of Economics and Magdalen College, Oxford. He became a barrister in 1955 and established a broad-based commercial practice. He was appointed Queen's Counsellor in 1975, a recorder of the crown court in 1977 and a circuit judge in 1982. He imposed stiff sentences for cases of violence, especially against women. When he retired in 1997 he was a senior judge at Southwark Crown Court, one of the busiest criminal courts in the country. After retirement, he acted as an arbitrator and recommended specialist judges for customs and excise cases. He married Stella Isaacs and had three children.

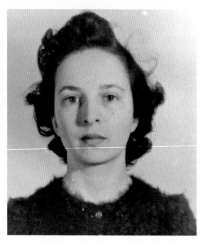

Muriel Byck

Special Forces heroine

1918–1944

Muriel Tamara Byck was born in Ealing, London. Her father, Jacques Byck, was a Jew from Kiev, Russia. Her mother, Luba née Besia, was from Lvov, Russia. Byck spent part of her childhood in continental Europe. From 1923–1924 the family lived in Wiesbaden, Germany, and from 1926–1930 in St Germain, France, where she attended a French *lycée*. Byck completed her degree at the French Lycée in Kensington, London, and then embarked on further study at Lille University. Byck's parents separated and she settled in England, moving to Torquay with her mother. In 1942 Byck joined the Women's Auxiliary Air Force (WAAF), rising to section officer. Owing to her fluency in French and working knowledge of Russian, she was recruited into the SOE. She trained to become a wireless operator in 1943, first at Winterfold in Cranleigh, Surrey, then at Morar in Scotland, and finally at Thame Park, Oxfordshire. In April 1944 she was parachuted into France, where she worked as a wireless operator under the codenames "Michéle" and "Violette" for the Ventriloquist Circuit. Less than two months after arriving in France, Byck contracted meningitis and died. She was buried in Pornic War Cemetery in France.

Charles Clore

The "man with the golden touch"
1904–1979

Charles Clore was born in Mile End, London. He was one of seven children of Israel Clore, a Russian immigrant, and his wife Yetta Abrahams. In 1927 Clore bought the rights to a cinema film of a world championship boxing match, which he resold at a profit in South Africa. He went on to become one of the most successful businessmen of his time. He made an indelible impression on the British high street when he acquired the fashion chain Richard Shops, bookmakers William Hill, shoe shop Dolcis and jewellers Mappin and Webb. Clore also built up an impressive property portfolio which included the Park Lane Hilton. But there was more to Clore than just business; in 1964 he founded the Clore Foundation in order to support a wide range of philanthropic activities. He reputedly gave £1m to the Jewish state on the outbreak of the Six Day War in 1967. He received a knighthood in recognition of his philanthropy in 1971. Clore's name is now particularly associated with the visual arts. Following his death in 1979 the Clore Gallery was built at the Tate to house J.M.W. Turner's paintings, and completed in 1987. The Clore Foundation has distributed more than £50 million to charitable purposes over the past decade.

Andrew Cohen

Dubbed the "proconsul
of African nationalism"
1909–1968

Andrew Cohen was born in
Berkhamsted, Hertfordshire.
His father came from a wealthy
Jewish family and his mother
from a radical Unitarian family,
though Cohen himself did
not hold any religious faith. Cohen attended Malvern College
and Trinity College, Cambridge. In 1932 he joined the civil service
and transferred to the Colonial Office. In 1947 he was appointed
Undersecretary of State for the Colonial Office's African division
and advocated self-government and nationalising colonial rule.
In 1950, Cohen spearheaded the confederation of the Rhodesias
and Nyasaland, which was achieved three years later. In 1952,
Cohen was appointed Governor of Uganda with the task of laying
the foundations for independence. As governor, he successfully
reorganised the legislative council, which created the basis for a
representative parliament, and established the Uganda Development
Corporation to promote the industrial and economic development
of the country. He was knighted in the same year. In 1957 he was
appointed British representative on the Trusteeship Council at the
United Nations, a post that he held until 1960. In 1959, Cohen
published British Policy in Changing Africa, which proposed connecting
American aid to British schemes for developing east Africa. From
1964 until his death, Cohen was Permanent Secretary to the Minister
of Overseas Development.

Arthur Cohen

The first practising
Jew to graduate from
Cambridge University
1829–1914

Arthur Cohen was born in
London to broker Benjamin
Cohen and his wife Justina.
His paternal grandparents
had arrived in England from
Holland. His maternal uncle was Jewish community leader Sir Moses
Montefiore. After studying in Frankfurt, Cohen tried to attend
Cambridge University, but admission was problematic due to his
Jewish heritage. It was only with the help of his uncle and the Prince
Consort that Cohen was able to attend Magdalene College in 1849.
He served as President of the Cambridge Union in 1853, despite
his Jewish background. Cohen had to wait until 1856 to graduate
as it was only then that the obligatory Christian oath, made upon
graduation, was removed. He was thus the first professing Jew to
graduate from Cambridge. A year later Cohen was called to the
bar and specialised in commercial law. He was appointed Queen's
Counsel in 1874. In 1880 he was elected Liberal MP for Southwark.
He was also Chairman of the Bar Council. He served as Vice-
President of Jews' College from 1892–1901. He had a prestigious
ministerial career and was made Privy Councillor in 1905. Cohen was
president of the Borough Jewish schools and President of the Board
of Deputies.

Benjamin Louis Cohen

Politician and Jewish
community leader
1844–1909

Benjamin Louis Cohen was born
in Finsbury, London. He was the
eighth of nine surviving children
of wealthy stockbroker Louis
Cohen and his wife, Rebecca
Floretta Keyser. Educated at
home, he went into the family firm of Louis Cohen & Sons in the
City. In 1870 he married his third cousin, Louisa Emily Merton, and
they had a daughter and three sons. Cohen was elected Tory MP
for East Islington in 1892 and a member of London County Council
from 1889–1901. With a house in Hyde Park Gardens and a country
house near Sevenoaks, Cohen's lifestyle was that of an English
country gentleman. He was a governor of several City hospitals
and orphanages and was created a baronet in 1905. He was on the
board of two Anglo-Jewish communal institutions, becoming Vice-
President of the United Synagogue and President of the Jewish Board
of Guardians at a time when mass immigration from eastern Europe
was putting the board's resources under strain. Cohen was an early
supporter of Jewish settlement in Palestine but in contrast felt that
Jewish immigration to Britain should be restricted and on a selective
basis.

Hannah Floretta Cohen
Philanthropist and civil servant
1875–1946

Hannah Floretta Cohen was born in Kensington and was the only daughter of stockbroker and Conservative MP Sir Benjamin Louis Cohen and his wife, Louisa Emily Merton. She had three brothers. The Cohen family were part of a network of wealthy families who provided the lay leadership of Anglo-Jewry until the mid-20th century. Cohen was educated at Roedean School and Newnham College, Cambridge. Although she had an independent income, she worked in the factory department of the Home Office during the First World War, moving to the Treasury from 1917–1920. She was one of the first women to be employed at a senior level in the civil service and was awarded an OBE for her work. In 1900, Cohen was the first woman elected to the Jewish Board of Guardians (JBG), becoming Honorary Secretary in 1921, Vice-President in 1926 and President from 1930–1940. Originally state help for the Jewish poor had been rejected, but Cohen appealed for funding in order to improve housing, health and convalescent facilities. She served on various governing bodies, including those of Roedean and Newnham College.

Myrella Cohen
Family lawyer and Judge
1927–2002

Myrella Cohen was born in Manchester. Her parents were the children of eastern European immigrants. She was educated at Manchester High School for Girls, Colwyn Bay Grammar School and Manchester University.

She became a barrister in 1950 and was the first woman barrister in Newcastle in 1953. Her appointment as Assistant Recorder in Teesside in 1967 made her the first woman in the north-east to hold judicial office. In 1970 she became the second Jewish woman to be appointed Queen's Counsel, and only the fifth woman overall. On her appointment in 1972 as the North-East Circuit Judge and High Court Family Division Deputy Judge, she was the country's third woman and youngest judge. Among her high-profile cases were the child abuse allegations in Cleveland in 1987. On moving to London in 1989, she sat at the Old Bailey and then at Harrow Crown Court. Myrella was strongly committed to her religious faith and was proud that she never compromised her observance throughout her career. She was a member of the Chief Rabbi's working party, which produced the prenuptial agreement used in the United Synagogue, and was instrumental in bringing reform to English law by tying civil divorce to agreement on religious divorce.

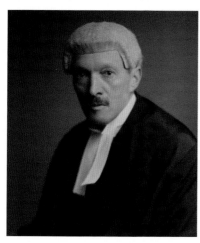

Lionel Cohen

Corporation lawyer, judge
and communal leader
1888–1973

Lionel Cohen was born in
London to a long-established
Anglo-Jewish family. He was
educated at Eton and New
College, Oxford. He became a
barrister in 1913 and developed
a large practice specialising in company law. He was appointed King's
Counsel in 1929 and was recognised as an authority in his field. In
1943 he was appointed as one of the five judges of the Chancery
Division and received a knighthood. In 1946 he was promoted to
the court of appeal and made a life peer in 1951 as Baron Cohen
of Walmer. He was appointed a lord of appeal in ordinary, retiring in
1960. He was the architect of the 1948 Companies Act and chaired
the royal commissions on awards to inventors and on taxation of
profits and income. He was a proud Jew and held many communal
positions including President of the Jewish Board of Guardians
and of the Jewish Historical Society, Vice-President of the Board
of Deputies and Chairman of the legal group of the Friends of the
Hebrew University. While retaining membership of the West London
Synagogue, Lionel became President of the Union of Liberal and
Progressive Synagogues. He was an excellent golfer and member of
nine golf clubs.

Ernst Joseph Cohn
Professor and barrister
1904–1976

Ernst Joseph Cohn was born in Breslau, Germany. His Jewish parents were Max Cohn, a merchant, and Charlotte, née Ruß. Educated in his home town, Cohn studied law at the University of Leipzig from 1922. In 1925 he attained his doctorate degree with a thesis that dealt with "problems of communications of declarations of intention through the medium of messengers". Cohn became a Rechtsreferendar in his home town until 1929 when, from the University of Frankfurt, he qualified as a court judge. Cohn was a professor at Kiel (1930–31) and Breslau (1932). As a Jew he was forced to leave Germany after the Nazis came to power, settling in England in 1937 and working as a barrister and lecturer. Cohn served in the British army during the Second World War. He continued lecturing at various universities both in England and abroad. In 1957 the University of Frankfurt finally managed to restore Cohn's position there, making him an honorary professor for German and English private and civil law. A board member of the British section of the World Jewish Congress, Cohn received honorary doctorates from the Universities of London and Cologne.

David Daube
Jurist
1909–1999

David Daube was born in Baden, Germany, to father Jakob, a wine merchant, and mother Selma, née Ascher. Both parents were Orthodox Jews. Daube was educated at Berthold Gymnasium and studied law at Freiburg University. There he came to the attention of German-Jewish jurist Otto Lenel, the founder of the modern study of Roman law. Although retired, Lenel tutored Daube personally and Daube attained a distinction for his doctorate in 1932. His thesis was based on Old Testament law so couldn't be published under the Nazis' ruling. Daube would have to wait 30 years to receive his degree. In 1933 Daube was compelled to leave Germany, settling in England alongside his mentor, Lenel. Daube gained a doctorate in Roman law at Cambridge in 1936 and would teach at various colleges from 1938–51. Daube's first book, *Studies in Biblical Law*, was published in 1947. In 1951 he became Professor of Jurisprudence at Aberdeen, having turned down a post at the Hebrew University of Jerusalem. His 1956 paper "Rabbinic Judaism" proved to be his most substantial, but in 1959 Daube wrote a well-regarded paper on Roman law, which became one of his lasting contributions to the field. Daube was Regius Professor of Civil Law at Oxford, 1955–70, and became the most noted of Roman lawyers. He was a fellow of the British and Bavarian academies and was awarded multiple honorary degrees. In the 1980s he settled in California.

Morris Harold Davis
Led the Stepney Borough
Council
1894–1985

Morris Harold Davies was born in the Jewish East End of London. He was raised in an Orthodox Jewish household by his eastern European parents. Davis was educated in several London County Council schools before taking up an apprenticeship with a tailor. In 1928, Davis became the leader of the Federation of Synagogues. Simultaneously, he was establishing a foothold in the Stepney Central Labour party, fashioning himself as the heir to its original secretary and Jewish immigrant, Oscar Tobin. He became the Vice-President in 1923 and the finance committee chairman in 1928. His controversial leadership of the Stepney Borough Council began in 1935 and lasted for nine years. Davis was a passionate Zionist and this was influential on his administration. He also formed an alliance on the council with the Irish Catholics, but this became problematic in the light of the Spanish Civil War during which most East End Jews sided with the Spanish republicans. Davis' political career ended in ignominy; in 1944 he was imprisoned for identity fraud (a ruse to avoid paying a rail fare) and did not return to public life.

Peter George Davis

Founding father of the SBS
1923–2011

Peter George Davis, known as "Pug", was born in Paddington, west London. He was educated at Highgate School, where he became a member of the cadet force and joined the Royal Marines (RM) in 1942. He trained at Chatham in the use of landing craft, and became known as the founding father of the Special Boat Service (SBS), a sister unit to the SAS. The name Special Boat Section was given by Pug to an RM Demolition Unit, which he established in post-war Germany. He created the sixth SBS in Malta to operate in the Mediterranean. The SBS went on to become the SB Company in 1959 with Pug in command. Pug saw service in Malaysia and then became second-in-command of the Joint Services Amphibious Warfare Centre. He taught amphibious warfare doctrine at the Joint Warfare Establishment before he retired in 1971. Pug was an active supporter of the Bournemouth Reform Synagogue and became Vice-Chairman of the Association of Jewish Ex-Servicemen. He received the Distinguished Service Order during the Second World War.

Frank de Pass

Victoria Cross winner
1887–1914

Frank Alexander de Pass was born in Kensington, London, to a family of Spanish and Portuguese Jews who originally came to England in the 1660s. His father was a West India merchant. He was educated at Abbey School, Beckenham and at Rugby. He attended the Royal Military Academy at Woolwich and was commissioned into the Royal Horse Artillery in 1906. In 1909 he joined the 34th Prince Albert Victor's Own Poona Horse, which was part of the Indian army. Posted to France during the First World War, de Pass was awarded the Victoria Cross for his bravery. He attacked a fortified German position and later rescued wounded men under fire during the fighting at Festubert on 24 November 1914. He was killed the next day as he tried to repair trench defences. De Pass was the first Jew to receive the Victoria Cross and the first Indian army officer to win the award in the First World War. He was buried at Bethune Town Cemetery and is commemorated on the Bevis Marks Synagogue war memorial in London and on a paving stone in Victoria Embankment Gardens.

Henry De Worms

MP who battled antisemitism
within politics
1840–1903

Henry De Worms was born in
London to Solomon De Worms,
a baron of Austria, and his
wife Henrietta. His paternal
grandfather had come from
Frankfurt and his grandmother
was Nathan Mayer Rothschild's sister. Henry was educated at King's
College, London. He was called to the bar in 1863 but left soon
after to work in his father's tea business. In 1867 De Worms stood
as the first Jewish Conservative candidate, competing for the seat
at Sandwich. This drew criticism from his Jewish acquaintances as
traditionally the Conservatives had opposed greater civil and political
freedom for Jews. He was unsuccessful in his bid, due in large part to
the antisemitic campaign of the Liberal party. In 1880 he was elected
MP for Greenwich and five years later won the seat at East Toxteth,
Liverpool. He had a successful career, serving as Parliamentary
Secretary to the Board of Trade. De Worms served as President of
the Anglo-Jewish Association, but resigned in 1886 after his daughter
married out of the faith. He served as MP for East Toxteth to 1891,
then as Undersecretary for the Colonies from 1888–92. He was the
first professing Jew to hold ministerial office in a Tory government,
and was created 1st Baron Pirbright in 1895. In 1901 he was left off
a list of influential Jews wishing to congratulate the new King George
VII and this may have been what finally cut his ties to Judaism. He
later requested a Christian burial.

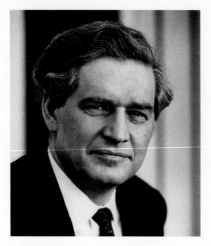

Edmund Dell
MP and Minister of State
1921–1999

Edmund Dell was born in London
to carnival goods manufacturer
Rueben Dell and his wife Frances.
As a child, Dell was London Boy's
Chess Champion. He served
in the Royal Artillery during
the Second World War and
then studied history at Oxford, where he became a member of the
Communist Party. Dell first worked in the dye manufacturing industry
in Manchester before turning to politics. In 1964 he was elected
Labour MP for Birkenhead. In 1966 he was made Parliamentary
Secretary at the Ministry of Technology before moving to the
Department of Economic Affairs a year later. As Minister of State at
the Board of Trade in 1968, Dell supported Robert Maxwell's "I'm
Backing Britain" campaign. The idea was to encourage the public to
buy British goods from British businesses. In 1974, Dell attempted
to strengthen Britain's beleaguered economy as Paymaster General
at the Treasury. He introduced the petroleum revenue tax, which
demanded a better share from North Sea oil companies. In 1979 Dell
left politics and pursued various business interests. He was director
of Shell Transport and Trading Co. and Channel 4's first chairman
in 1980. In 1996 he wrote his economic history *The Chancellors: A
History of the Exchequer, 1945–90.*

John Diamond
MP and Chief Secretary
1907–2004

John "Jack" Diamond was born in Leeds to parents Solomon and Henrietta. The family was observant and Solomon was a rabbi. In 1931 Diamond qualified as a chartered accountant and established his own firm, John Diamond and Co. He also became Managing Director of Capital and Provincial News Theatres, which was a high-street cinema chain specialising in screening newsreels. He is best known as a Labour politician and first stood for election in 1945. He won his seat in Blackley, Manchester, during the Labour landslide under Clement Attlee. He again won a seat with Labour in the 1957 Gloucester by-election and was appointed Chief Secretary to the Treasury, a Cabinet position, in 1964. Six years later he was appointed Baron Diamond of Gloucester and held a number of government advisory positions. He was defeated at the 1970 election, and then appointed a life peer. He later joined the Social Democratic Party and was its leader in the Lords. Diamond was active in Jewish social affairs and established the Cambridge and Bethnal Green Jewish Boys Club.

Benjamin Disraeli
The first Jewish Prime Minister
1804–1881

Benjamin Disraeli was born in London to novelist Isaac D'israeli and his wife Rebecca. Both parents had Italian-Jewish ancestry but were not particularly observant. Benjamin and his siblings were baptised into the Church of England as children. Disraeli first stood for parliament in 1832 as an independent candidate. He later joined the Tory party and stood for three constituencies. He served as Chancellor of the Exchequer and Leader of the Commons in minority Conservative governments in 1852, 1858 and 1867–8. In 1868 Disraeli became Prime Minister in a minority Conservative government, but his party was defeated at the 1868 general election. It was, however, elected with a large majority in 1874, with Disraeli serving as Prime Minister from 1874–80. In 1876 he was made Earl of Beaconsfield by Queen Victoria. He was a novelist of note, and is famous for his parliamentary battles with his great rival, William E. Gladstone. Disraeli was the first man of Jewish birth to be elected Prime Minister. However, due to English law, if he had not been baptised he would not have been able to stand for parliament at all. Disraeli remained respectful of his Jewish heritage, a sentiment that was augmented by a visit to Jerusalem in 1830.

Coningsby Disraeli
Conservative politician
1867–1936

Coningsby Disraeli was born in
Kensington, London. His father,
Ralph Disraeli, was the brother
of Prime Minister Benjamin
Disraeli. Coningsby was the last
in the male line of the Disraeli
family. He was educated at
Charterhouse School and New College, Oxford. Upon his father's
death in 1898, he inherited his uncle's mansion, Hughenden
Manor in Buckinghamshire. Coningsby Disraeli was an officer in the
Buckinghamshire Yeomanry. He entered parliament during the 1892
general election, and sat as Conservative MP for Altrincham from
1892 until he was defeated in the 1906 election, along with many
other Tory MPs. He did not return to politics thereafter, but served
as the High Sheriff of Buckinghamshire from 1931–2. He lived a
quiet and solitary life in Hughenden until his death, after which the
property was acquired by the National Trust.

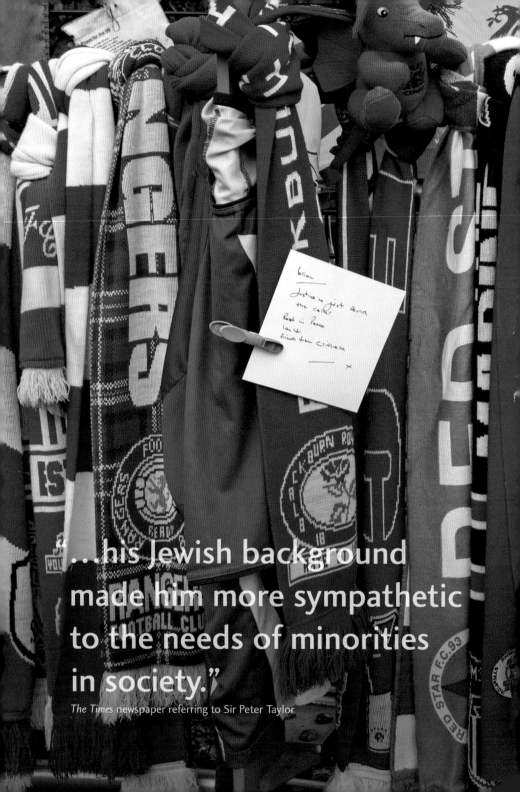

"...his Jewish background made him more sympathetic to the needs of minorities in society."

The Times newspaper referring to Sir Peter Taylor

Jews and the
Legal Profession

Sir Peter Taylor was commissioned by the
government to undertake an inquiry into the
Hillsborough football disaster. The Taylor Report
he produced led to the introduction of all-seater
stadiums at top English football clubs.

Passing through the gates to the Inner Temple Courts, London, 1937

Jews and the Legal Profession

Professor William D. Rubinstein
Historian and Author

The Jewish profile of England's legal profession, probably until the Second World War, was very different to what it was on the European continent. In central Europe before Hitler, Jews comprised an extraordinary percentage of law students and of practising lawyers, with 54 per cent of lawyers in Berlin and 61 per cent of lawyers in Vienna in 1933 being Jews.

These figures – which were fully exploited by the Nazis – had no parallel in England. In 1883, only 47 solicitors in London out of a total of 4,920, less than one per cent, were Jews. About two per cent of barristers in England at that time were Jews. These percentages did not rise significantly until the 1930s, when the sons (and daughters) of the wave of Jewish migrants from eastern Europe began to enter the professions.

Before the later 19th century, anyone who wished to practise law in England had, theoretically, to swear the required oath, which included the words "on the true faith of a Christian". When the first Jewish lawyers appeared, they were allowed to omit these words from the oath, and there is no record of any Jew not being allowed to practise law in Britain because of their religion. Early would-be Jewish lawyers did, however, suffer from a number of *de facto* barriers. Most barristers attended Oxford or Cambridge Universities, for example, before enrolling at one of the Inns of Court. There, at such institutions as the Oxford Union Debating Society, they often learned the arts of public speaking, quick-wittedness and the ability to convince in debate required of any successful barrister. But prior to 1855, anyone matriculating (formally enrolling) at Oxford or graduating from Cambridge had to sign a statement of agreement with the Thirty-Nine Articles of the Anglican religion, which effectively excluded professing Jews (as well as Protestant Nonconformists and Roman Catholics) from either university. Barristers were also required to appear in most courts on Saturdays and Jewish holidays, while those who went on circuit (travelling to local courts throughout England and Wales) had the additional problem of finding kosher food. The small Jewish community in England (numbering 37,000 in 1850) was heavily oriented towards the commercial trades, and as yet had few professional men in its ranks.

The first Jewish barrister in England was Sir Francis Goldsmid, 2nd Baronet (1808–78), who was called to the bar at Lincoln's Inn in 1833. He was the son of the millionaire financier Sir Isaac Lyon Goldsmid, 1st Baronet (1778–1859) and thus had ample means and personal contacts to ensure professional success. He also became the first Jewish QC (Queen's Counsel), in 1858 – the same year that professing Jews were first allowed to sit in parliament. Goldsmid retired the following year, and was himself elected to parliament in 1860. To avoid appearing in court on Saturdays, Goldsmid practised in the court of chancery, which had more flexible hours. The first Jew to appear regularly in the common law courts was the Jamaica-born Sir John Simon (1818–97), who also became a QC, in 1868.

Like Goldsmid, most of the early Jewish barristers came from wealthy, highly acculturated families, such as Sir George Jessel (1824–83), who was educated at the secular University College London and became probably the highest paid barrister in the country when he was appointed solicitor general by Prime Minister William E. Gladstone in 1868. Jessel was appointed Master of the Rolls (one of the most senior judges) in 1873, the first Jew to be appointed a judge in Britain. He was known for his relatively rapid judgments, in contrast to the notorious slowness of previous judges, satirised by Charles Dickens and others. A rather unusual QC of that time was Judah P. Benjamin (1811–84), who had served, improbably, as Secretary of State of the confederate states during the American Civil War, and then fled to England to escape possible prosecution for treason. In London, he became a leading barrister and a QC in 1872. Two judges of this period who were of Jewish descent might also be mentioned. Farrer Herschell, 1st Baron Herschell (1837–99), was the son of a Polish Jew who became a conversionist missionary to the Jews in London. Herschell served as Lord Chancellor (the most senior judge in Britain and a member of the Cabinet) in 1886 and 1892–95. Sir Archibald Levin Smith (1836–2001), whose mother was Jewish, served as Master of the Rolls in 1900–01. Levin Smith had a glandular disorder that caused him to grow to seven feet tall – a rather intimidating judge!

The period from about 1890 until the Second World War was arguably the golden age of famous English barristers, some of whom, like F.E. Smith (later Lord Birkenhead) and Sir Edward Marshall Hall, became household names. At that time, lengthy reports of murder and divorce cases were printed in the British press, and the lawyers involved became well known. Probably the best known Jewish barrister of that time was Sir Rufus Isaacs (1860–1935), the son of a London fruit merchant; he became a barrister after an unsuccessful career as a stockbroker. A leading Liberal MP and a QC from 1898, Isaacs acted in many famous cases and was once paid the unusual compliment by F.E. Smith that Isaacs "was quite as clever as I am." After serving in the Cabinet he was appointed lord chief justice in 1913, retiring from that post in 1921. Just before this he was prominently named as one of the alleged beneficiaries of the so-called "Marconi Scandal",

Gilbert Beyfus defended the famously flamboyant entertainer Liberace
(pictured above) against the *Daily Mirror* who suggested he was gay

involving "insider trading" about a government contract, which also nearly ended the career of David Lloyd George. Isaacs was attacked in antisemitic terms, especially after being named Lord Chief Justice. From 1921 till 1926 he served as Viceroy of India, the only Jewish viceroy, and was made Marquess of Reading, the only Jew to hold so senior a rank in the peerage. Isaacs' second wife, Stella Charnaud (1894–1971), who was not Jewish, in 1958 became the first woman to sit in the House of Lords, as Baroness Swanborough.

Only a few Jews achieved real fame as barristers in the early post-1945 period. One who did was Gilbert Beyfus QC (1885–1960). His most famous case came in 1959 when he acted for Liberace, the American entertainer, who sued the *Daily Mirror* for suggesting that he was gay, illegal at the time. Beyfus was successful, and Liberace received damages of £8,000, a record at the time. After Liberace's death in 1987, it was revealed that everything the newspaper had said about him was true.

Prior to the 1940s, few Jews had been appointed as judges; but since then there have been a significant number. Sir Lionel Cohen, Baron Cohen (1888–1973), was appointed a judge in 1943 and a senior judge in 1946. Other Jewish judges of the time included Sir Seymour Karminski (1907–74); Cyril Barnett Salmon, Baron Salmon (1902–91); and Sir Alan Mocatta (1907–90). In the past few decades, a remarkable number of Jews have been appointed to the most senior judicial positions. Among these were no fewer than three lord chief justices, Sir Peter Taylor, Baron Taylor of Gosforth (1930–97); Sir Harry Woolf, Baron Woolf (b.1933); and Sir Nicholas Phillips, Baron Phillips of Worth Maltravers (b.1938). In addition, the current President of the Supreme Court of the UK (established in 2009) is also Jewish, Sir David Neuberger, Baron Neuberger of Abbotsbury (b.1948), as were three other lords of appeal in ordinary, senior appeals judges. This is an extraordinary record for a community numbering half of one per cent of the British population. Several have become widely known, for instance Sir Peter Taylor, whose Yiddish-speaking parents migrated from Lithuania; he was the author of the Taylor Report, which investigated the tragic Hillsborough football disaster of 1989, in which 96 Liverpool fans died.

In recent years, as well, several Jewish barristers have achieved great political success, among them Michael Howard QC (b.1941); Sir Malcolm Rifkind QC (b.1946); and Leon Brittan QC (1939–2015), all of whom held senior Cabinet positions in Conservative governments, with Howard serving as Leader of the Conservative party from 2003 to 2005. Samuel Silkin QC (1918–88) served as Attorney General in the 1974–79 Labour government.

Another aspect of the Jewish contribution to the legal profession that might be noted is the considerable contribution of immigrant and refugee lawyers who settled in Britain, such as Sir Hersch Lauterpacht (1897–1960), who spoke almost no English when he arrived in 1923, but became Whewell Professor of International Law at Cambridge and a leading judge in the International Court of Justice.

The first Jews to become solicitors in Britain are believed to have been Joseph Abrahams in 1770 and Joshua Montefiore (uncle of the famous Sir Moses) in 1784. The number of Jewish solicitors was initially small, and grew only slowly until after the First World War, when the number of Jewish solicitors grew rapidly. It has since continued to grow.

Probably the earliest prominent Jewish solicitor in England was Sir George Henry Lewis, 1st Baronet (1833–1911), who became well-known in several high-profile cases before becoming a close friend and confidant of the Prince of Wales (later Edward VII), as well as of many figures in London high society. He is also known for formulating the Moneylender's Act of 1900, which regulated trade.

Several prominent Jewish solicitors and firms have had major connections with the literary and artistic world. One of the most prominent is Rubinstein, Nash & Co., founded by Joseph Samuel Rubinstein (1852–1915) and carried on by his son Stanley Rubinstein (1890–1976) and relative Michael Rubinstein (1920–2001). Among the well-known literary cases in which they were involved were, in 1928, defending (unsuccessfully) the lesbian novel by Radclyffe Hall, *The Well of Loneliness,* and, in 1960, acting (successfully) for the publishers of the unexpurgated edition of D.H. Lawrence's *Lady Chatterley's Lover.* Among the partners in the firm – he later quit to found his own firm – was Arnold Goodman, Baron Goodman (1913–95), the extraordinary "Mr Fixit", who served as Prime Minister Harold Wilson's right-hand man during the 1960s and became one of the most famous, if mysterious, public figures of his time. Goodman served as Chairman of the Arts Council (1964–72) and as Master of University College, Oxford (1976–86). After his death, it was alleged that he was, despite his name, a bad man, who had embezzled large sums of money from a trust account. His firm paid £500,000 to the alleged victim "without admission of guilt."

As with Jewish barristers, several Jewish solicitors have held senior positions in British governments. Harry Louis Nathan, 1st Baron (1889–1971), served in the Attlee Labour government in the House of Lords as Undersecretary of State for War (1945–6) and Minister for Civil Aviation (1946–8). He was also the legal advisor to the British Zionist Organisation. Lewis Silkin (1889–1972), a Labour MP from 1936 to 1950, and then a peer as 1st Baron Silkin, from 1945 to 1950 served as Minister of Town and Country Planning. In that post, he was responsible for many very important initiatives, such as the New Towns Act of 1945, which created the "new towns", and the Access to the Countryside Act of 1949, which created the national park system. His son John Silkin (1923–87), also a solicitor, held office in the Wilson and Callaghan governments.

Another notable solicitor who served in the Labour Party was Victor Mishcon, Baron Mishcon (1915–2006), who was a shadow spokesman for Labour in the House of Lords from 1983 to 1992. He was the founder of Mishcon da Reya, among the best-known firms of solicitors in Britain. One of the firm's most visible members is Anthony Julius (b.1956), who acted as solicitor for Princess Diana during her divorce from Prince Charles and for Deborah Lipstadt, in the famous lawsuit brought in 2000 by Holocaust denier David Irving. Julius has also written widely on the history of antisemitism.

Prior to 1919, although women could become doctors or university lecturers in Britain, they were debarred from becoming lawyers. In that year – a year after women aged 30 or older were given the vote – parliament passed the Sex (Removal of Disqualifications) Act 1919, one of the least-known major pieces of social legislation in British history. In a few sentences, it removed all legal barriers to women entering any profession, including the law. Initially, however, few women became lawyers. The first Jewish barrister was Sara Moshkowitz, in 1925. Born in Kishinev, Russia, she later moved to Israel and practised there under a different name. Probably the best-known Jewish women barristers were Dame Rose Heilbron (1914–2005) and Dame Rosalyn Higgins, Baroness Higgins (b.1937). Heilbron, who was called to the bar in 1939, was responsible for a string of "firsts" for any woman. She was the first (of two) female KCs, in 1939 (at the age of only 34); the first woman to lead in a murder trial; and, in 1965, became the first woman judge of the high court. Baroness Higgins became a member of the International Court of Justice in 1995, and served as its president from 2006–9.

Lewis Silkin's brainchild Milton Keynes was formally designated as a 'new town' in 1967

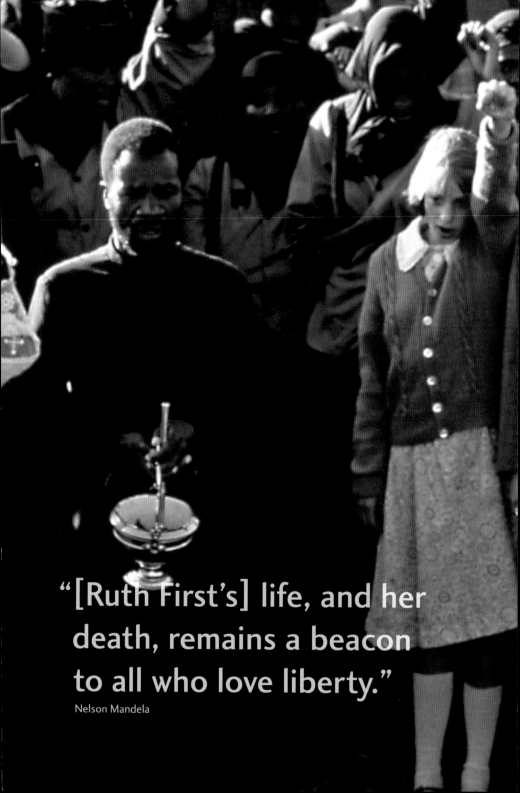

"[Ruth First's] life, and her death, remains a beacon to all who love liberty."
Nelson Mandela

Biographies E – K

A World Apart is a 1988 anti-Apartheid drama, written by Shawn Slovo, daughter of Ruth First, based on the lives of Slovo's parents, Ruth and Joe Slovo.

Harry Errington
George Cross winner
1910–2004

Harry Errington was born in Soho, London, to Polish immigrants Solomon and Bella Ehregott, who anglicised their surname shortly before Errington was born. Attending Westminster Free School, Errington won an engraver scholarship. The nitric acid involved in the work affected his chest, so Errington became a tailor for his uncle, opening a shop on Savile Row and becoming a master tailor. In 1939, with war imminent, Errington volunteered as an auxiliary fireman on Shaftesbury Avenue. In 1940, during an air raid, Errington and others were trapped in a basement after a direct hit that killed 20 people. Errington carried a fellow fireman outside, taking him to safety, but returned into the fire to rescue another comrade, risking the loss of his hands, which were badly injured. Within months, all three men were back on fire duty. In 1941, Errington received the George Cross for his actions, one of only three firemen to receive this honour in the Second World War. In 1948, Errington oversaw the basketball competition in the London Olympics, and became a life vice-chairman for the sport. Errington was also an honorary treasurer of the VC and GC Association.

Morris Finer
Judge and social reformer
1917–1974

Morris Finer was born in the East End of London. He was educated at Teesdale Elementary School, Kilburn Grammar School and the London School of Economics. He became a barrister in 1943 and supplemented his income writing articles for the *London Evening Standard*. Gradually he built up a flourishing company practice, authored the standard textbook on company law and became a Queen's Counsel in 1963. He represented The Beatles in the 1960s and the Pilot's Union after the Trident disaster. He is well-known for the reports of two important committees he chaired. The first report, Justice for All, recommended making good legal advice accessible through local law centres. The second, which looked at the problems of one-parent families, was a landmark report with recommendations for family courts working with the social security authorities and for opportunities for conciliation. In 1972 he was appointed a judge of the high court, family division, and in 1974 he chaired the Royal Commission on the press but died suddenly aged 57. Morris married Edith Rubner in 1943 at Hampstead Synagogue and closely identified with Israel, supporting the Society of Lawyers and Accountants for Aid to Israel. He enjoyed good food and drink and long walks in the countryside.

Ruth First

Lifelong friend of
Nelson Mandela and
anti-apartheid activist
1925–1982

Ruth First was born in
Johannesburg, South Africa. Her
parents were Jewish immigrants
from Latvia who founded the
Communist Party of South Africa.
First was educated at Jeppe High School for Girls and the University
of the Witwatersrand. Her time on campus was politically formative;
she helped found the Federation of Progressive Students and began a
lifelong friendship with Nelson Mandela. First and her husband joined
the African National Congress and in 1956 she was among the 156
anti-apartheid activists arrested and accused of treason. In 1963 she
was imprisoned for 117 days without charge. First later published a
book in which she detailed the brutal interrogation techniques used
on her, including isolation and sensory deprivation. She was exiled to
London in 1964 and settled in Camden, but continued to be a vocal
anti-apartheid activist in addition to her academic work. Her final
research post was at the Eduardo Mondlane University in
Mozambique. It was there, in 1982, that she was assassinated by a
parcel bomb sent by order of a South African police major. First has
since between portrayed in two films, *A World Apart* (1988) and *Catch
a Fire* (2006).

Gerry Flamberg
War hero and anti-fascist
campaigner
1922–2007

Gerald Flamberg was born in
Holborn, London, to a Polish-
Jewish father, Jacob, and British
mother, Miriam, née Beaver.
Flamberg left school at 14 to
become a fishmonger. In 1941 he
enlisted into the King's Royal Rifle Corps before joining the 156th
Parachute Battalion. He served in North Africa, Sicily and mainland
Italy. In 1944 Flamberg fought in Operation Market Garden, where
he was wrongly ordered into the path of a German tank, sustaining
a shoulder injury. He crawled back to safety, but his unit was pinned
down by the tank's fire. Flamberg asked for permission to attack
the tank with a Gammon bomb and, without the use of his injured
arm, forced the tank to retreat. Flamberg earned the Military Medal
for his actions, but was captured in battle at Arnhem. As a POW in
Brunswick, Flamberg organised pledges from prisoners and officers
to make donations to the working-class poor in London, and in 1949
all the funds were paid into the Brunswick Boys Club, inaugurated
by Prince Philip. From 1946 Flamberg fought as part of 43 Group
against the rise of Mosley's fascism in England, changing his surname
to Lambert due to safety concerns.

Henrietta "Netta" Franklin
Educationist and suffragist
1866–1964

Henrietta "Netta" Franklin was born in London. Her father, Samuel Montagu, was a prominent Jewish leader as well as a wealthy banker, and was created 1st Baron Swaythling. Her mother was Ellen Cohen. She was educated at Doreck College and King's College for Ladies, London. Franklin's meeting with educational reformer Charlotte Mason in 1890 led to her starting the first Parents' National Educational School in London in 1892. Although her father and husband were both Orthodox Jews, Franklin supported her sister Lily Montagu's vision for reforming British Judaism and helped to establish liberal Judaism. Franklin was a committed suffragist and was active in numerous liberal and feminist causes. She was one of the founding members of the Jewish League for Woman Suffrage in 1912 and later served as President of the National Union of Women's Suffrage Societies. During the First World War she was a pacifist who supported the Women's International Congress at The Hague in 1915, which demanded an alternative solution to war and that women should have a voice in national affairs. After suffrage was gained in 1918, Franklin's attention turned to welfare legislation for women. She was President of the National Council of Women from 1925 to 1927.

Hugh Franklin

Civil liberties activist
1889–1962

Hugh Arthur Franklin was born in London. He was the fourth child of banker, Arthur Franklin, and his wife Caroline Jacob. His parents were Jewish and he was raised in the faith. He was educated at Clifton College and Gonville and Caius, Cambridge. Both his mother and his aunt, Henrietta Franklin, were involved in the suffrage movement and Franklin joined the Men's League for Women's Suffrage. During this time he lost his religious faith. In 1910 he joined the Men's Political Union for Women's Enfranchisement (MPU), and missed most of his final exams at Cambridge due to helping organise the Women's Social and Political Union "From Prison to Citizenship" procession on 18 June 1910. Franklin was arrested but not charged during the Black Friday deputation to parliament in November 1910 and later attempted to whip the Home Secretary, Winston Churchill, whom he believed to be responsible for the police brutality. Franklin was imprisoned in Pentonville for six weeks and went on hunger strike. Subsequent imprisonments led to him being force-fed. His second marriage in 1921 to Elsie Constance Tuke caused his father to disinherit him for marrying out of the faith. Franklin continued to fight for civil rights, becoming Treasurer of the National Council for Civil Liberties from 1934–39.

Anna Gaitskell
Labour Life Peer
1901–1989

Anna Dora Creditor was born near Riga, Latvia, then part of imperial Russia, to Leon, a Hebrew scholar, and Tessa (née Jaffe). Following Leon in 1903, the family emigrated to Stepney Green, London. Gaitskell won a scholarship to Coborn High School for Girls and joined the Labour Party at the age of 16. In 1933 she followed her lover, fledgling Labour politician Hugh Gaitskell, to Vienna. The couple married in 1937 and had two daughters together. In 1945, Hugh Gaitskell was elected MP for Leeds South East and eventually became leader of the Labour Party. Anna became politically active in her own right and was an outspoken champion of human rights and libertarian causes. She enjoyed a substantial political career of her own and, following her husband's death in 1963, was made a life peer. The following year, Prime Minister Harold Wilson appointed Gaitskell as Delegate to the United Nations where she was vocal in her advocacy of the needs of the third world, countering what she perceived as the hypocrisy prevalent in certain African and Asian countries. Gaitskell had a firm commitment to the state of Israel, yet criticised some of the right-wing policies of the Likud government.

Robert Gee
Victoria Cross winner
1876–1970

Robert Gee was born in Leicester
to English-born parents of Jewish
descent. He was apprenticed
at 16 to an ornamental and
metal ironworks but left to
join the Royal Fusiliers. He
studied military history and
was appointed a lecturer. In 1915 he joined the Second Battalion
of the Royal Fusiliers as a temporary captain. He fought in Gallipoli
and Egypt, becoming Staff Captain, 86th Brigade. He was wounded
in 1916, was awarded the Military Cross and went to serve at the
Somme. He was awarded the Victoria Cross for his conspicuous
bravery, initiative and determination in November 1917 when he and
brigade headquarters were captured by the enemy. Gee escaped,
killing an enemy soldier in the process, then organised a party of
brigade staff, followed by two infantry companies, to counter-attack.
They cleared the area and established a defensive flank. Gee then
captured an enemy machine gun, killing eight of its crew, and
organised the brigade's defence, despite being wounded. Gee was
also mentioned in dispatches three times for his bravery. After
the war, Gee entered politics and became a Conservative MP for
Woolwich East, 1921–22 and for Bosworth, 1924–27. Disillusioned
with politics, he emigrated to Australia. He was a first-class sportsman
in hockey and cross-country running.

Albert Goldsmid

Colonel and communal leader
1846–1904

Albert Goldsmid was born at Pune, Bombay, India to Henry Edward and Jess Goldsmid. When his father died in 1854, the family returned to England. Goldsmid was educated by private tutors and at the Royal Military Academy, Sandhurst. He became a career officer in the army, rising through the ranks to become a colonel in 1894. Albert served with distinction in the Boer War (1899–1902). He was the highest ranking Jewish officer in the British army in the 19th century and was awarded the MVO by the King in 1903. While Albert's father and maternal grandfather had converted to Christianity, he converted to Judaism aged 24. He became a keen Zionist and was chief of the Chovevei Zion of Great Britain, promoting a Jewish return to the land of Israel. He founded the Jewish Lads' Brigade and became President of the Maccabeans, a Zionist friendly society. He was Honorary President of the Cardiff Hebrew Congregation and is buried at the Willesden United Synagogue Cemetery, London.

Francis Henry Goldsmid
Britain's first Jewish barrister
1808–1878

Sir Francis Henry Goldsmid, 2nd Baronet, was born in London to financier Isaac Goldsmid and his wife Isabel. His father had been raised in an Orthodox house but was a firm supporter of Jewish emancipation. Francis wholly shared his father's views. In 1833 Goldsmid was called to the bar and became the first practising Jew to be appointed a barrister. In 1858 he became the first Jew to be created Queen's Counsel. Two years after Observant Jews were allowed to sit in the House of Commons, Goldsmid was elected as MP for Reading. He served this constituency until his death. He was given the nickname "member for Jewry" due to his vocal support for greater Jewish civil freedom. Goldsmid was also a leading figure in the Jewish community. In 1840 he played a role in the establishment of the Reform movement and in the opening of the West London Synagogue. A year later he founded the first Jewish infants' school, which grew to be the largest in England. In 1871 he established the Anglo-Jewish Association, partly in response to the Board of Deputies' decision to exclude Reform Jews, but also to further the cause of Jewish emancipation.

Frederick David Goldsmid

Banker and philanthropist
1812–1866

Frederick David Goldsmid was born in London to financier Isaac Goldsmid and his wife Isabel. His father had been raised in an Orthodox house but came to believe that Jews should change their religious practice in order to achieve greater civil freedoms. His sons also advocated this view and became involved in the Reform movement. Goldsmid studied at University College London. He then joined his father's company Mocatta & Goldsmid, successful bullion bankers to the Bank of England. In 1865 Goldsmid was elected as MP for Honiton, a post in which he served until his death. He was a member of the Metropolitan Association for Improving Dwellings of the Industrious Classes. A forerunner of the modern Housing Association, they campaigned for better housing for the working class, with a return for private investors. Goldsmid was also active in Jewish affairs, supporting the Jews' Hospital and the West Metropolitan Jewish School. The latter was attached to the West London Synagogue, where Goldsmid's brother Francis was also an active member.

Isaac Lyon Goldsmid

Founding member of the
West London Synagogue
of British Jews
1778–1859

Isaac Lyon Goldsmid was born
in London, the eldest son of
Asher Goldsmid, a bullion broker,
and his wife Rachel Keyser. He
was educated at Dr Hamilton's
school in Finsbury Square, before going to work for the family firm of
Mocatta & Goldsmid, bullion brokers to the British government. In
1806, Goldsmid became a stockbroker. He made most of his wealth
as a loan broker to foreign states, and later became a director of the
London, Brighton and South Coast Railway. Goldsmid became active
in the cause of anti-slavery and reform of the penal system, and
also played a leading part in founding the non-sectarian University
College London in 1826. He was also a huge advocate for Jewish
emancipation and social reform, and was one of the founders and
leading members of the West London Synagogue of British Jews in
1842, the first Reform congregation in Britain. In 1830, Goldsmid
helped to introduce the Jewish Disabilities Bill in the House of
Commons, which, although unsuccessful at the time, was eventually
passed in 1859. In 1841, Goldsmid was made a baronet, becoming
the first professing Jew to receive an English hereditary title.

James d'Avigdor-Goldsmid

British army officer and
Conservative politician
1912–1987

James Arthur d'Avigdor-Goldsmid
was born into the wealthy Anglo-
Jewish d'Avigdor-Goldsmid family.
His father, Sir Osmond d'Avigdor-
Goldsmid, 1st Baronet, was the
President of the Board of Deputies of British Jews and Chairman for
the Jewish Agency for Palestine in London. James d'Avigdor-Goldsmid,
who succeeded to his father's baronetcy as 2nd Baronet, was
educated at Harrow School, followed by the Royal Military College,
Sandhurst. He was then commissioned into the 4th/7th Royal
Dragoon Guards in 1932 and was promoted to captain by 1940,
participating in the D-Day landings of the Second World War. He
was awarded the Military Cross for his service in 1944. d'Avigdor-
Goldsmid was promoted to major in 1946, lieutenant colonel in
1951 and colonel in 1956. In 1965, he was appointed President of
the Regular Commissions Board and a year later, was posted to the
Ministry of Defence as Director of Territorial Army and Cadets. He
was appointed Companion of the Order of the Bath (CB) in the 1965
Queen's Birthday Honours for his military service. In 1968, d'Avigdor-
Goldsmid retired from the military, and moved into the political arena.
He was elected as the Conservative MP for Lichfield and Tamworth in
1970, but lost his seat in the October 1974 general election.

Julian Goldsmid
Politician and community leader
1838–1896

Julian Goldsmid was born in London to Frederick Goldsmid and his wife Caroline Samuel. He studied at University College London, graduating with a master's in Classics in 1861. He was later elected fellow of the college and was called to the bar. Goldsmid practised law briefly before standing for parliament. He was elected as MP for Honiton in 1866. This was the seat his father had held for many years. However, Goldsmid lost his position when Honiton was disfranchised by the 1867 Reform Act. He successfully stood for two other seats, in Rochester and St Pancras South, holding the latter until his death. In 1894 Goldsmid was appointed Deputy Speaker of the House of Commons and was known for his knowledge of parliamentary proceedings. Active in Jewish affairs, Goldsmid was Vice-President of the Anglo-Jewish Association and Chairman of the Russo-Jewish Committee. He was able to draw attention to the plight of eastern European Jews, who were facing much persecution. He was also Preacher and Warden of the West London Synagogue. As Director of the London, Brighton and South Coast Railway, Goldsmid had a steam locomotive named after him in 1892.

Louisa Goldsmid

Feminist and campaigner
for women's education
1819–1908

Louisa Sophia Goldsmid was born into a wealthy Anglo-Jewish family. Her father was Moses Asher Goldsmid and her mother Eliza Salomons. She married her first cousin, Francis Henry Goldsmid, (later 2nd Baronet), who helped to establish Reform Judaism in Britain, and she shared his religious and social views.Goldsmid was an early campaigner for women's rights and her family were all involved in the education of women and the rights of British Jews. Through her mother-in-law, Isabel Goldsmid, Goldsmid met Emily Davies. The friends were involved in the founding of Girton College, Cambridge in 1869. Goldsmid was a member of the first Women's Suffrage Committee in London but temporarily withdrew in her efforts to secure the vote for women. She believed that the suffrage petition to J.S. Mill should be restricted to demand the vote for unmarried and widowed women and that the goal of complete equality was hopeless. Goldsmid's focus was then on women's education and in 1887, she took part in the movement to allow women to take Cambridge degrees. In later life, she became an executive committee member of the National Society for Women's Suffrage.

Arnold Goodman

The government's go-to lawyer

1915–1995

Aby Goodman was born into an Orthodox family in London. His father, Joseph, was a master draper and his mother Bertha completely doted on her son, who changed his name to Arnold during the Second World War. In 1933 Goodman graduated with a law degree from University College London. During the war he enlisted in the Royal Artillery. His commander, Mortimer Wheeler, described him as "the greatest quartermaster-sergeant in the history of the army". In 1954 Goodman established his own legal practice with Henry Derrick. Goodman Derrick represented many figures from the media and arts. However, Goodman made his name in 1957, working on the famous *Spectator* libel case. He represented three Labour politicians accused of perjury after having denied they had been drunk at an International Socialist Congress. Goodman was successful and soon became the Labour government's go-to lawyer. He worked for Harold Wilson, successfully keeping Labour's legal matters out of the media. In 1965 Goodman was created a baron and was appointed Chairman of the Arts Council of Great Britain. He was President of the Union of Liberal and Progressive Synagogues as well as the Jewish Chronicle Trust.

Thomas William Gould
Victoria Cross winner
1914–2001

Thomas (Tommy) William Gould was born in Dover. His father was killed in action in 1916 during the First World War. Gould was educated at St James School, Dover. He joined the Royal Navy in 1933 and the submarine service three years later. Tommy was a petty officer in the Royal Navy when he won the Victoria Cross for bravery in the face of the enemy. Tommy and Lieutenant Roberts successfully removed unexploded bombs that had landed inside the casing on the deck of HM Submarine *Thrasher* in 1942. After the war he became a business consultant and personnel manager of Great Universal Stores. He became a lieutenant with the Bromley Sea Cadets and was elected President of the International Submarine Association of Great Britain. Tommy helped to found the 43 Group to fight fascism and became Vice-President of the Association of Jewish Ex-Servicemen (AJEX). He supported the Zionist cause, marching through London in 1946 in protest at the Labour government's policy towards the Jews in Palestine. In 1987 Tommy auctioned his VC via Sotheby's because of financial hardship. It was bought by AJEX for £48,400.

Eugene Grebenik

Helped develop demography
in Britain
1919–2001

Eugene Grebenik was born in
Kiev, Ukraine to liberal Jewish
parents. In 1920, the family
moved to Germany. Following
the rise of Hitler they settled in
England in 1933. Grebenik was
educated at the Xaverian College in Brighton, and obtained a first-
class honours degree in economics from the LSE. In 1940, he became
a lecturer at the LSE and contributed to the 1946 National Survey
of Health and Development cohort study. He was promoted to LSE
Reader in Demography in 1949. One of his greatest achievements
was his work with David Glass on the 1946 Royal Commission on
Population, whichis considered to be a landmark study of cohort
analysis. From 1954, he was a professor at Leeds University and
became joint editor with David Glass of *Population Studies* in the same
year. In 1970, he became the first principal of the new civil service
college at Sunningdale and served on the "Population Panel" set up
by the government. During this time he also helped to develop the
human sciences degree at the University of Oxford, which included
compulsory modules in demography. He left the college in 1976 to
work at the Office of Population Censuses and Surveys, where he
prepared the major demographic reviews of 1977 and 1984. In an
ironic twist of fate, this great demographer's birth was not registered,
as Grebenik's mother wished to conceal him from the Bolsheviks'
attempt to "nationalise" babies.

Louis Hagen
War hero, writer, film producer
1916–2000

Born in Potsdam, Germany, Louis Hagen was known to his family as Büdi, the diminutive of brüderlein (little brother). The son of a banker, whose real family name was Levy, he grew up in a modernist villa built by his father. At 15 he was denounced for writing an anti-Nazi joke on a postcard and deported to Schloss Lichtenburg concentration camp, until he was rescued by the father of a school friend. In 1936 he left for England, where his circle of left-wing friends included Jennie Lee and Aneurin Bevan. When war broke he joined the Pioneer Corps with the alias "Lewis Haig", a necessity for anyone of German origin in case of capture. He flew a glider in the Arnhem landings and was awarded the Military Medal. His bestselling book *Arnhem Lift* (1945) was published anonymously due to army opposition. Transferred to India in 1945, despite wishing to see the liberation of Europe, he worked for a military newspaper, and was the first Western journalist to interview Ho Chi Minh. After the war, he wrote books, including *Indian Route March* (1946) and *The Secret War for Europe* (1969), and produced 25 children's films with his childhood art teacher, the celebrated animator Lotte Reiniger.

Percy Alfred Harris
Politician
1876–1952

Percy Harris was born in London, the son of Wolf Harris, a Polish born merchant of Bing, Harris & Co., who traded with New Zealand. He was educated at Harrow and Cambridge and was then called to the bar. He did not practise, instead becoming head of the family firm and an expert on New Zealand politics. Harris enjoyed a lengthy career as a significant figure in the Liberal Party. He served as a member of the London County Council from 1907–34 and from 1946 until his death, and was its deputy chairman from 1915–16. He also served in parliament, as MP for Market Harborough from 1916–18 and for Bethnal Green from 1922–45, often as the only Liberal MP in a London seat. On the radical wing of the Liberal Party, he served as its deputy leader from 1940–45. Harris was created a baronet in 1932. Although his father had been a warden of the New West End Synagogue, Harris had an Anglican funeral. His non-Jewish wife Freda née Bloxam was one of the designers of the standard deck of Tarot cards.

Rose Heilbron
Britain's first female judge
1914–2005

Rose Heilbron was born in Liverpool. Her paternal grandparents were from Germany and the USA. She was educated at Belvedere School, Liverpool and Liverpool University. She was the first woman to be awarded a Lord Justice Holker scholarship to Gray's Inn. She became a barrister in 1939 and was elected to the northern circuit. In 1949 she was one of the first women to be appointed King's Counsel and she was the first woman to take the lead in a murder case. Helibron was one of the most successful defence advocates of her day and in 1956 she was appointed Recorder of Burnley and England's first woman judge. In 1972, she became the first woman to sit as a judge in the Old Bailey. In 1974, she became only the second female high court judge and was made Dame of the British Empire. In 1978 she was made presiding judge on the northern circuit – the first woman Presiding Judge of any circuit. In 1985 she was elected Treasurer of Gray's Inn, the first woman to be treasurer of any of the four Inns of Court. Rose had a strong Jewish identity and was active on behalf of many Jewish and Israeli causes. She was also a keen golfer.

Farrer Herschell
Lord Chancellor of Great Britain
1837–1899

Farrer Herschell was born in Brampton, Huntingdonshire to Ridley Haim Herschell and Helen Skirving. His father, who was originally from Prussian Poland, had converted from Judaism to Christianity and helped found the British Society for the Propagation of the Gospel Among the Jews, so Farrer was raised as a Christian. He was educated at a grammar school in south London, followed by the University of Bonn, and University College London, where he graduated with a degree in Classics. However, his true vocation was for the law, and he was called to the bar at Lincoln's Inn in 1860. Herschell started out on the northern circuit with no connections and had to supplement his income by contributing to the *New Reports* (1863–5). He took silk in 1872 and served as Recorder of Carlisle from 1873–80. In 1874, Herschell moved into the world of politics and became a Liberal MP for Durham City, a seat he held until 1885. He was appointed solicitor general by Prime Minister William Gladstone in 1880, and was knighted soon after. He was appointed Lord Chancellor of Great Britain in 1886 and created 1st Baron Herschell. He served again in the same role from 1892 to 1895. He was awarded the Knights Grand Cross of the Order of the Bath in 1893.

Ellis Hillman
Barnet's first Labour mayor
1928–1996

Ellis Hillman was born in West Hampstead, London. His parents were Scottish Jews. Hillman was evacuated to Rickmansworth in 1939, but would return home every week for the Sabbath. Two years later his father let him return home permanently on the condition that he commuted back to Rickmansworth School to finish his education. In early life Hillman was a member of the Revolutionary Communist Party and of the Revolutionary Socialist League. In 1958, Hillman joined the London County Council and was a leading member until 1981. In 1973, he became the Chairman of the Arts and Recreation Committee in Labour's Greater London Council administration, weathering the storm of the inflation crisis and its attendant spending cuts. Hillman was elected as a Councillor for Barnet in 1986 and in 1994 its first Labour mayor. He was passionate about subterranean London and published an illustrated work, *London Under London*, in 1985. Hillman was an atheist, but observed Jewish tradition and greeted everyone he met with "shalom". He was also the founder and President of the Lewis Carroll Society as well as a supporter of the Flat Earth Society.

David Hirsch

Victoria Cross winner

1896–1917

David Hirsch was born in Leeds, Yorkshire. He was appointed head boy at Willeston School, Nantwich, where he excelled both as a scholar and as an all-round athlete, taking more wickets for the school than any previous bowler and holding the record for the mile. On leaving school in 1914 Hirsch won an open exhibition to Worcester College, Oxford, but war intervened and he joined the Leeds University Officer Training Corps. In 1915 he was transferred to the Yorkshire Regiment (The Green Howards) where he rose to Captain. His battalion fought at the Battle of the Somme and he was wounded at Eaucourt L'Abbaye. On 23 April 1917 Hirsch was wounded twice during the Battle of Arras. Despite this he returned over fire-swept slopes to ensure that his battalion's defensive flank was being established. Under intense machine gun fire he moved continuously up and down the line encouraging his men to dig in and hold their position. He continued to encourage his men by standing on the parapet and steadying them in the face of more machine gun fire and counterattack until he was killed. He was 20 years old and his body was never found. Hirsch was awarded the Victoria Cross posthumously "for most conspicuous bravery and devotion to duty in attack". His name is listed on the Memorial to the Missing at Arras. His parents paid for a swimming pool in his memory at his former school, and a plaque was placed on Leeds City Art Gallery. His Victoria Cross is on display at the Regimental Museum of the Green Howards in Richmond, North Yorkshire.

Rufus Isaacs
The only Jewish viceroy
1860–1935

Rufus Isaacs was born in London to fruit importer Joseph Isaacs and wife Sarah. His great-uncle was the famous boxer Daniel Mendoza. Isaacs was called to the bar in 1887 and was appointed Queen's Counsel in 1898. In 1904 he was elected Liberal MP for Reading. Six years later Isaacs was appointed to the post of Attorney General. It fell to him to prosecute Emmeline Pankhurst despite being in favour of votes for women. Both Isaacs and his ally Lloyd George were embroiled in the Marconi scandal, when highly placed members of the Liberal government were accused of insider trading with the Marconi Company, where Isaac's brother Geoffrey was chairman. Historians have explored the possibility of antisemitism in the allegations, but there was enough substance in them to threaten Isaacs' career. But he recovered sufficiently to become Lord Chief Justice in 1913. In 1917, Isaacs was sent to America to seek closer cooperation within the war effort. He was extremely successful and Lloyd George commented that the country could not do without him. A year later, he was named Ambassador-Extraordinary and High Commissioner at Washington. After the war, Isaacs became viceroy of India. He supported eventual Indian self-rule but had Gandhi arrested for sedition in 1922. He worked hard at balancing competing national interests and had a hand in the transfer of power to India later in his career. In 1926 Isaacs was created a marquess, the only Jew to be granted this honour. He served as Foreign Minister in 1931.

Barnett Janner
Politician and prominent
Anglo-Jewish figure
1892–1982

Born in Lucknick, Lithuania
(then in the Russian Empire),
Barnett Janner moved to Barry,
south Wales, when nine months
old. He won scholarships to
Barry County School and
the University College of South Wales and Monmouthshire. He
was articled to a firm of Cardiff solicitors before joining the Royal
Artillery Garrison. Despatched to France in 1917, the following year
he suffered a mustard gas attack, and was nearly killed. Following
the Armistice, Janner entered politics and stood unsuccessfully
as a Liberal candidate for Cardiff council and then for a Cardiff
constituency in 1929, before moving to London. He was elected for
Whitechapel in 1931, but lost the seat to Labour in 1935. A lifelong
Zionist, he highlighted the plight of German Jews, and founded the
Parliamentary Palestine Committee. His political views moved to the
left, and in 1936 he joined the Labour Party. He served as an ARP
warden during the Second World War, then in 1945 was elected for
the Leicester West Constituency, a seat he held until 1970. He served
as a member of the Board of Deputies of British Jews and of the
executive of the English Zionist Federation. He was knighted in 1961,
and created a life peer in 1970.

George Jessel
The first practising Jew to
hold a ministerial position
1824–1883

George Jessel was born in
London to diamond merchant
Zadok Aaron Jessel and his
wife Mary. He was educated
at Mr Neumegen's school for
Jews in Kew before studying
at University College London. Jessel was called to the bar in 1847
and applied to become a Queen's Counsel in 1861. He was not
successful on his first attempt, but was appointed QC four years
later. In 1868 Jessel was elected Liberal MP for Dover. Upon hearing
Jessel speak in the House of Commons, Gladstone was so impressed
he appointed Jessel Solicitor General. It is thought that he was the
first practising Jew to hold a high ministerial position. In 1873 Jessel
was made Master of the Rolls. In this position he also served as Chief
Judge in the court of appeal. He was known for his quick and precise
judgments and it was said he could read both sides of a piece of
paper at the same time! Jessel was a Hebrew and biblical scholar and
Vice-President of the Anglo-Jewish Association.

Dudley Joel

Conservative MP who was killed
in action during the Second
World War
1904–1941

Dudley Joel was born in London.
His father, Solomon Joel, had
made a fortune in gold and
diamond mining in South
Africa. Solomon worked with
his brothers in the Barnato Diamond Mining Company and was also
very successful in the world of horse racing. His wife, Ellen Ridel, had
converted to Judaism upon their marriage and the family was very
observant. Joel was educated at Repton School and King's College,
Cambridge. He then worked in London as an insurance underwriter.
In 1931 he inherited Moulton Paddocks in Newmarket, a horse racing
centre formerly owned by Sir Ernest Cassel. In the same year, he
successfully stood as Conservative candidate for Dudley. He was
re-elected in 1935. In 1941 he was killed while serving with the Royal
Navy Volunteer Reserves. His ship, *Registan*, was bombed by German
aircraft near Cape Cornwall. Joel died along with 63 other crew
members. He was buried in Willesden Jewish Cemetery. There is now a
shield in the House of Commons chamber to commemorate his death.

Keith Joseph
Cabinet Minister and
Thatcher's mentor
1918–1994

Keith Joseph was born in
London to businessman Samuel
Joseph and wife Edna Cicely.
His father had been Lord
Mayor of London. The family
attended London's Liberal
Synagogue and Joseph remained observant throughout his life. He
studied law and joined the Young Conservatives in 1948. In 1956
he was elected MP for Leeds North-East, and became one of only
two Jewish Tory ministers. He held several government positions
including Minister for Housing and Local Government and Secretary
of State for Social Services. Joseph is best known as the intellectual
force behind Thatcherism. In 1974 he established the Conservative
Centre for Policy Studies. Its aim was to bring together politicians
who desired economic and social change, forming a new "common
ground." He favoured privatisation and free market liberalism. Joseph
also championed new social policies such as widely available birth
control for single mothers. These ideas sparked much controversy.
In 1975 he began a campaign to be the new Tory leader but later
backed Margaret Thatcher. Many of his ideas came to pass through
her leadership. Joseph was an extremely private person but was once
voted one of the top 10 best-dressed men in Britain.

Otto Kahn-Freund
Academic lawyer
1900–1979

Otto Kahn-Freund was born in Frankfurt-am-Main to a cultured Jewish family and was educated at Goethe Gymnasium and the Universities of Frankfurt, Heidelberg and Leipzig. He became a judge of the Berlin labour court and came as a refugee to England when dismissed by the Nazis in 1933. Kahn-Freund joined the London School of Economics as a student and became an assistant lecturer and a barrister in 1936. He naturalised in 1940 and became a professor in 1951. He became a leading authority on labour law in England. In 1964 Otto became Professor of Comparative Law at Oxford and a fellow at Brasenose College. In 1965 he became a Fellow of the British Academy and was appointed to the Royal Commission on the reform of the trade unions and employers' associations. He was made Queen's Counsel in 1972 and was knighted in 1976. He was a regular contributor to the *Modern Law Review* and he published many of his own works. Kahn-Freund was an agnostic but he attributed his love of justice and identification with the disadvantaged to his Jewish identity. This, he believed, lay behind his involvement in labour law and his socialist convictions.

Seymour Karminski
High Court judge
1902–1974

Seymour Karminski was born in Hampstead, London. He was the son of a German-born bank manager and educated at Rugby school and Christ Church, Oxford. Called to the bar at the Inner Temple in 1925, Karminski became King's Counsel in 1945. During the Second World War, he served in the Royal Navy, and was made lieutenant commander in 1943. Karminski specialised in divorce cases and was appointed Judge of the Divorce Division of the high court of justice in 1951, making him one of the two Jewish judges on the high court bench at the time. He received the customary knighthood in 1951, and was made a privy councillor in 1967. In 1969, Karminski was promoted to Lord Justice of Appeal, an office that he held until 1973. Outside of his legal duties, Karminski was an active figure in the Jewish community. He served as Chairman of the London Jewish Board of Guardians and was a prominent member of the West London Reform Synagogue.

Gerald Kaufman
Father of the House of Commons
1930–2017

Gerald Kaufman was born in Leeds. His parents, Louis and Jane, came from Poland before the First World War. He was educated at Leeds Grammar School before studying philosophy, politics and economics at Oxford. Prior to his career in politics, Kaufman was a journalist for the *Daily Mirror* and the *New Statesman*. Kaufman was elected Labour MP for Manchester Ardwick in 1970. He worked in the Department of Industry and as Shadow Environment Secretary before being elected MP for Manchester Gorton in 1983. Kaufman served as Shadow Home Secretary and Shadow Foreign Secretary. In 2009 he became embroiled in the expenses scandal, having billed for an expensive rug and a TV among other items. Kaufman argued his obsessive-compulsive disorder was the reason behind the claims. In 2015, he became Father of the House of Commons, the longest-serving active MP. Kaufman was a member of the Jewish Labour Movement. He was deeply critical of Israel, comparing it to apartheid South Africa and calling for economic sanctions. These controversial views were anathema to many in the Jewish community.

Michael Kerr
Lord Justice of Appeal
1921–2002

Michael Robert Emmanuel Kerr was born in Berlin. His father, Alfred Kempner, was an author and critic, and his mother, Julia, née Weisman, was a pianist and composer. In March 1933 Kerr and his family fled the Nazis, eventually settling in Paris. Kerr was educated at the Lycée Michelet, where he won the Prix d'Excellence. He described the accolade later as "probably my greatest achievement ever". Moving to London in 1935, Kerr studied at Clare College, Cambridge in 1939. A year later he was interned as an enemy alien for six months before joining the RAF, flying Wellington bombers in 1944. Returning to Cambridge to complete his studies, Kerr attained a double first in law. Joining a leading firm, he took silk in 1961, becoming a Queen's Counsel, and was one of the bar's top earners by the 1970s. In 1972 he was appointed a judge of the high court and knighted. He reluctantly accepted the chair of the Law Commission in 1978, successfully handling the legal issues surrounding membership of the European Economic Community. In 1981 Kerr was appointed Lord Justice of Appeal. He oversaw 1981's Criminal Attempts Act and 1985's Enduring Power of Attorney Act. In 1991 he was awarded Germany's Commander's Cross of the Order of Merit.

Leonard Maurice Keysor
Victoria Cross winner
1885–1951

Leonard Keysor was born in Paddington, London to English-born parents. He was educated at Townley Castle, Ramsgate, and emigrated to Canada in 1904 and Australia in 1914. On the outbreak of the First World War, he joined the Australian Imperial Force, serving in Egypt and then Gallipoli. During the battle of Lone Pine in August 1915 Leonard's courageous actions won him a Victoria Cross. As Turkish bombs were thrown into his trench, he smothered them with sandbags or threw them back, sometimes catching them in mid-flight. Despite being twice wounded he continued his efforts for 50 hours. His actions saved the trench. He returned to England to recover from fever and then continued serving until the end of the war. In 1920 he returned to London, entered business and married Gladys Benjamin at Hill Street Synagogue. Leonard was a member of the Liberal Jewish Synagogue, St John's Wood. His Victoria Cross was among items stolen from his flat in 1920 but returned by post the following day with an apology note. Leonard re-enacted his bomb-throwing exploits in the 1927 film, *For Valour*.

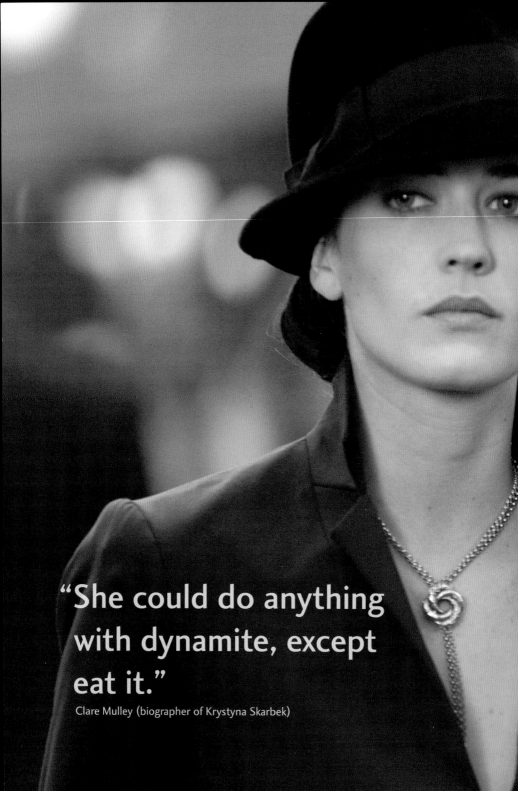

"She could do anything with dynamite, except eat it."

Clare Mulley (biographer of Krystyna Skarbek)

50 Shades of
Charlotte Gray...

It has been said that Ian Fleming based
the character Vesper Lynd, seen here
portrayed by Eva Green in *Casino
Royale*, 2006, on Krystyna Skarbek.

Memorial to members of the Special Operations Executive,
Albert Embankment, London

50 Shades of Charlotte Gray: Remembering the contribution of the Jewish Female SOE Agents of the Second World War

Clare Mulley
Author

Denise Bloch worked as a secretary at Citroën in France. Muriel Byck was an assistant stage manager in a London theatre. Krystyna Skarbek was a rather bored Polish countess smuggling cigarettes across borders on her skis for kicks, and Vera Rosenberg worked as a translator and rep for an oil company in Romania. Aside from being Jewish, or having Jewish heritage, these women seemed to have little in common. With the advent of the Second World War, however, all four would be recruited by Britain's Special Operations Executive, or SOE, the secret organisation established in July 1940 to support sabotage and armed resistance behind enemy lines, and launched with Churchill's instructions "to set Europe ablaze".

A truly pioneering organisation, SOE selected agents solely on the basis of their ability and commitment. At a time when women in the forces were prohibited from carrying arms, SOE quietly put men and women through the same training, including silent killing and the use of guns and explosives, and sent them to work alongside each other in the field. Although SOE had a disproportionately high number of Jewish agents, given the demographic as a whole, Krystyna was one of only three female special agents with Jewish heritage, alongside Denise Bloch and Muriel Byck. All three would make a significant contribution to the Allied war effort. Unknown to many however, there was another Jewish-born woman in the organisation. Vera Rosenberg, or Vera Atkins as she became known, worked closely with Maurice Buckmaster, the head of SOE's French or F-Section, the largest country section in the organisation, but she kept her identity hidden.

Krystyna Skarbek was born in Warsaw in 1908. Her father, the handsome but fickle scion of a noble Polish family, had married a Jewish banking heiress to cover his debts. "Listen Count and take heed, not to step into debt", ran one scurrilous antisemitic song at the time. "It may land you in a stew, having as a wife, the daughter of a Jew." Although brought up a Roman Catholic in a wealthy household, Krystyna's Jewish roots, and later conversion to Protestantism to secure an early divorce, meant she was never fully accepted in the higher echelons of Polish society, and she was determined to prove herself from a young age.

Krystyna was en route to her second husband's diplomatic posting in southern Africa when Nazi Germany invaded their homeland in September 1939. By the time she got back to Europe it seemed too late to volunteer for her country. Instead Krystyna found her way to the supposedly anonymous offices of the British Secret Services and demanded to be taken on. With her language skills, contacts and knowledge of the smuggling routes into Europe's first occupied country, despite being a foreign national, Jewish on her mother's side and a woman, she was immediately taken on. Before the end of the year she would be living under an alias in Budapest, preparing to smuggle money and propaganda in to the fledgling Polish resistance and bring back radio codes to establish communications, along with information on Wehrmacht troop movements. Her value to the Allies was confirmed when in 1941 she also brought out the first microfilm evidence – hidden inside her gloves – of preparations for Operation Barbarossa, the Nazi German invasion of the Soviet Union. Arrested and interrogated more than once, Krystyna always managed to keep her cool and talk her way out of danger, even helping to save the fellow officer arrested with her on separate occasions in Poland and Hungary.

Vera Atkins joined SOE in London in early 1941 while Krystyna was still working undercover in Europe, and in a sense Vera arrived already undercover herself. Born Vera Rosenberg in Romania to a German-Jewish father and British-Jewish mother, in 1940 Vera adopted an anglicised version of her mother's maiden name, Etkins, as she fled rising antisemitism. That spring she travelled first to the Low Countries, where she supplied the money to bribe an Abwehr officer for a passport for her cousin. After going into hiding when the Nazis invaded the Netherlands that May, she finally reached Britain with the help of the Belgian resistance. Once in London Vera never revealed her true identity and, usually found in "a twin set or tweed", she looked the very model of a well-to-do Englishwoman just up from the country.

Vera quickly became an "invaluable assistant" to Maurice Buckmaster of F-Section. Had her illicit payment to a Nazi officer come to light, her position would certainly have been compromised. As it was, she was soon supporting the recruitment and deployment of agents in occupied France, and from 1942 she took responsibility for what would eventually become the 37 women sent into the field. Most agents found her formidable but, like Buckmaster, respected her judgement and valued her work arranging their cover stories, liaising with their families and managing their pay. She would come to know Krystyna, Denise and Muriel in London at different times.

Paris-born Denise had been 23 when the war broke out, and her father and two of her brothers served with the French army. Two of the men were taken prisoner, but the younger brothers managed to join the resistance. In July 1942 they and Denise left Paris for Lyon, escaping the infamous Vel' d'Hiv round-up of over 13,000 members of the Parisian Jewish community for transportation to Auschwitz.

British Type 3 Mk. II Second World War spy radio set, housed in an unobtrusive leather suitcase it allowed special forces agents operating on occupied territory to travel inconspicuously

On the way, they changed their family name from Bloch to Barrault. It was while she was working at Citroën in Lyon that Denise was recruited into the resistance, joining an SOE-supported network in the city. Despite some early criticism of her work, she served as a courier for several months and evaded arrest twice within 10 days after the circuit was penetrated by the Nazis, forcing her into hiding until early 1943.

Two years younger than Denise, Muriel had been born in Ealing, west London, to Russian-Jewish parents who had been living in France. It was her faultless French, along with her determination to serve, that eventually led to her enrolment with SOE in the summer of 1943. Muriel specialised in Morse and wireless work and so great was the need for wireless operators that with Vera's blessing she was parachuted into France before her training was officially complete. Although very security-conscious, cycling around the region to transmit from different locations and so elude the Nazi signal-detection vehicles, Muriel was nearly caught by pure chance when a curious German officer peered into the shed where she was sending a signal. Fortunately her fellow resistants managed to spirit her away. Not long later she narrowly avoided being caught in an early RAF bombing raid on a military target that she herself had helped organise.

Having changed her identity and dyed her dark hair blonde, in 1943 Denise left Lyon to support a circuit near Agen. She was soon tasked with bringing out information on the state of the resistance to Britain via a treacherous 15-hour hike over the Pyrenees and subsequent flight through Spain and Portugal. It was now that she was officially recruited by SOE in London, training as a wireless operator before being covertly returned to central France by a Special Duties Squadron Lysander in March 1944. Vera saw her off, giving her a last check over to make sure she hadn't left anything incriminating in her pockets. Over the next three months Denise exchanged over 80 wireless messages with London, arranging drops of guns, explosives and other supplies for the resistance circuit around Nantes.

Denise and Muriel had both now proved their worth, but it was increasingly clear that 25-year-old Muriel was not well. In mid-May 1944, less than a month before D-Day, she collapsed at a safe house. Claiming to be her uncle, her French circuit leader rushed her to hospital where a spinal tap confirmed meningitis. Muriel died in his arms that evening. She had sent and received over 40 signals in the six weeks of her active service, and was posthumously mentioned in dispatches. A few weeks after Muriel's death, Denise was arrested near Nantes.

After her cover had been blown in Hungary, Krystyna had been redeployed in Egypt and the Middle East, before being dropped behind enemy lines in southern France in the summer of 1944. Her achievements here would make her legendary in the special forces. Not only did Krystyna support the brilliant SOE circuit leader Francis Cammaerts to prepare for the Allied invasion in the south of France, she also independently made the first contact between the French resistance and the Italian partisans; secured the defection of a Nazi German garrison in a strategic pass in the Alps; and saved the lives of three fellow officers, including Cammaerts, just hours before their planned execution by firing squad.

After several months in detention, Denise was deported to Germany. Transported with her were two other F-Section female agents, Lilian Rolfe and Violette Szabo. The women reached Ravensbrück, the Nazi concentration camp for women north of Berlin, on 22 August 1944, just days before the liberation of Paris. After six months' hard labour all three women had lost their health and strength, and in late January 1945 they were moved to solitary cells. Then they disappeared.

Krystyna was in Paris to celebrate the liberation of the French capital. A few weeks later she hitched a flight back to London, where she begged to be returned to Poland. Vera summed her up as "very brave, very attractive, but a loner and a law unto herself". After a few weeks in Italy waiting for her Polish mission, which was eventually cancelled, Krystyna was back in Cairo in May 1945 when VE Day arrived.

After the war, Vera made it her personal mission, funded by MI6, to find out what had happened to all the agents who had not returned, and ensure that they were recognised. It was she who discovered that, sometime in late January/early February 1945, Denise Bloch, Lilian Rolfe and Violette Szabo had been taken into a courtyard near the Ravensbrück crematorium, Denise leaning on Violette as she was too weak to walk unaided. Each woman was then executed with a shot to the back of the neck. Denise was just 29. As a French citizen she was posthumously awarded the Légion d'Honneur, Croix de Guerre avec palme and the Médaille de la Résistance avec rosette. The British honoured her with the King's Commendation for Brave Conduct.

Unable to return to post-war Poland under a Soviet-backed Communist regime, Krystyna took British citizenship as "Christine Granville", the wartime alias of which, she said, she had become "so proud". She was honoured with the OBE, George Medal and French Croix de Guerre avec étoile in recognition of her courage and achievements. In 1952 Krystyna was murdered in South Kensington by Dennis Muldowney, a ship's steward who had formed an obsession with her. She was stabbed through the heart with a commando knife much like the one she had carried throughout the war.

Vera Atkins was also awarded the Croix de Guerre. Despite later controversy about her and Buckmaster continuing to send agents to France when it seemed likely that their circuits were compromised, leading to the capture and execution of several men and women, in the 1990s Vera was made a Knight of the Légion d'Honneur by the French government, and appointed CBE by the British. She died in 2000.

All too often women in the resistance or female special agents tend to be presented in romantic terms, as courageous and beautiful if perhaps not as effective as their male counterparts. In fact, they were a remarkably diverse group. Women who volunteered for service as couriers and wireless operators, running escape lines and leading partisan armies, were all courageous, fluent in at least one continental language and deeply committed to the Allied cause, but otherwise had little in common. As well as working women there were several aristocrats and one princess. Some were mothers, one a grandmother. Many were beautiful (which held its own advantages and risks), others plain, and one, the American Virginia Hall, had a prosthetic leg. Most were British or French, but they also came from the Soviet Union, Poland, Belgium, the Netherlands, Ireland, America, Switzerland, India, Australia and Chile, and two were from Germany. was a Muslim. Krystyna Skarbek, Denise Bloch and Muriel Byck were all Jewish, Krystyna at least on her mother's side. Although one woman was arrested on arrival in France, most of the female agents were effective, at least for a short while, and Krystyna was not only the first to serve Britain, but also the longest-serving, surviving six years in the field. However, the huge contribution of this diverse group of women came at a high price. Twenty-nine were arrested, 16 executed, and Muriel also died while serving during the war. All deserve to be properly remembered.

Opposite Virginia Hall, radioing London from an old barn near Le Chambon sur Ligon *Les Marguerites Fleuriront ce Soir*, Jeffrey W. Bass, 2006, oil on canvas

"The magnitude, the
mystery and the nature
is so well indicated by
that stirring name, the
Great Barrier Reef."
Matthew Nathan

Biographies L – N

London born Matthew Nathan served as the
Governor of Queensland from 1920–1925.
During his time in Australia he founded the
Great Barrier Reef Committee, to promote
research and conservation on the reef.

George Lane
Commando
1915–2010

George Lane was born Lanyi Dyuri in Hungary. His parents were landowners. At the age of four, the region Lane lived in was given to Czechoslovakia, turning his family into refugees. Schooled in Budapest, Lane was later a member of the Hungarian Olympic water polo team. In 1935 Lane went to London University before joining the Grenadier Guards at the start of the Second World War. Lane, however, was served with a deportation notice, spending a year in the Alien Pioneer Corps before his release, after which he joined the Special Operations Executive, serving in missions to Belgium and Holland. He joined X Troop, German-speaking soldiers, in 1943 and a year later led a pre-D-Day mission close to Ault during which he was captured trying to return to England. After interrogation, he was driven to meet Rommel, who, according to Lane, was a gentleman who saved him from being executed by the Gestapo. Lane escaped when taking sick POWs to a nearby hospital, and was later awarded the Military Cross.

Minnie Lansbury

Schoolteacher, East End
suffragette and rebel councillor
1889–1922

Minnie Lansbury was born in
Stepney to Isaac Glassman
and his wife Annie Goodkindt,
who were both Jewish migrants
from Poland. Minnie was a
schoolteacher who married
Edgar Lansbury, the son of politician George Lansbury, in 1914.
As a member of the National Union of Teachers, Lansbury was an
activist, demanding equal pay for women. She was part of the East
London Federation of Suffragettes (ELF), led by Sylvia Pankhurst,
and her husband became treasurer. The ELF combined the campaign
for suffrage with socialism, fighting for numerous causes to improve
conditions of the working class. Lansbury was elected to Poplar
council in 1919 and was one of 30 Labour councillors imprisoned in
1921 for their protest against unequal rate-setting between boroughs.
Her father-in-law and her husband were among those jailed.
Ultimately London County Council backed down and the councillors
were released after six weeks, but conditions in prison were poor and
Lansbury's health suffered as a result. She died from pneumonia on
New Year's Day in 1922 and was buried in East Ham Jewish Cemetery.

Harold Joseph Laski

Academic, political theorist and
chairman of the Labour Party
1893–1950

Harold Laski was born in
Manchester, the son of a Jewish
cotton merchant; his brother
Neville Laski was a leading figure
in the Anglo-Jewish community
with very different political views
from his brother. Harold Laski attended Manchester Grammar School.
Aged just, he married a gentile student in London, Frida Kerry, eight
years his senior. Laski later attended New College, Oxford. From
1916–20 he taught in America, returning to become an academic
at the London School of Economics, an institution with which he
was associated for the rest of his life. An unorthodox liberal Marxist,
Laski turned down several offers of safe Labour parliamentary seats,
but was a member of the party's National Executive Committee and
Chairman of the Labour Party from 1945–46. When Labour was
elected to power in 1945, he immediately entered into a public
dispute with Prime Minister Clement Attlee, suggesting that Attlee
had no right to become Prime Minister without the endorsement of
the party's National Committee, for which he was famously rebuked
by Attlee. Laski also, unwisely, sued the Daily Express for libel over
an allegation that he supported violent revolution. He lost the case
and with it much of his political influence. As a lecturer, Laski was
particularly influential with Third World students and intellectuals.
Although an agnostic and remote from the Jewish community, he later
became a strong supporter of the establishment of the State of Israel.

Neville Laski

Barrister, judge and
communal leader
1890–1969

Neville Laski was born and grew
up in Manchester. His father had
emigrated from Russian Poland as
a young child and his mother was
of Lithuanian ancestry. Laski was
educated at Manchester
Grammar School, Clifton College and Corpus Christi College, Oxford.
He practised as a barrister in Manchester and became a Queen's
Counsel in 1930 and moved to London. His main position in the
Jewish community was as President of the Board of Deputies from
1933–39, when he was instrumental in helping thousands of refugees
from the Nazis arrive. Neville was appointed Recorder of Burnley
(1935–56), Judge of Appeal of the Isle of Man (1953–56) and
Judge of the Crown Court and Recorder of Liverpool (1956–63).
He also served on the General Council of the Bar as Chairman of
its Professional Conduct Committee and honorary treasurer. In
Manchester he was Honorary Secretary of the Manchester Jewish
Communal Council, President of the Northern Federation of Jewish
Literary Societies and Chairman of the Manchester Victoria Memorial
Jewish Hospital. In London he acted as President of the Board
of Deputies of British Jews, Vice-President of the Anglo-Jewish
Association and a presiding elder of the Spanish and Portuguese
Jews Congregation. He wrote several books relating to Jewish
defence and the plight of German Jewry. The novelist Marghanita
Laski was his daughter.

Simon Latutin
George Cross winner
1916–1944

Shimeon Latutin was born in Camden, London. His master-tailor father, Moses Valtutin, was from Riga, Latvia and his mother, Fradel Kraftcheck, was from Poland. Latutin was educated at North London Polytechnic and won a Westmoreland scholarship to the Royal Academy of Music for violin, achieving the Certificate of Merit. In 1932 he was awarded a four-year Sainton Scholarship and the Bache Scholarship in 1935. At the age of 20, Latutin was playing viola for the London Symphony Orchestra. In 1940, Latutin was enlisted into the Auxiliary Military Pioneer Corps. Commissioned into the Somerset Light Infantry in 1942, Latutin served in Mogadishu, Somaliland. In 1944, now a captain, Latutin and two colleagues were choosing New Year fireworks in a store when a fire broke out, lighting up the large number of rockets and creating an inferno. Latutin dragged out a virtually unconscious officer and, despite being alight himself, re-entered the fire to rescue his other comrade. He had to be physically prevented from saving the last person still inside, and died of his injuries the following day. In 1946, Latutin was posthumously awarded the George Cross for his bravery.

Hersch Lauterpacht
International lawyer
1897–1960

Hersch Lauterpacht was born
in Zolkiew, Galicia and was
educated at the Universities of
Lemberg and Vienna. In 1923 he
came to England and attended
the London School of Economics.
He became an assistant lecturer
in 1927, Reader in the University of London in 1935 and Professor of
International law at Cambridge from 1938 to 1955. He was made a
barrister in 1936 and a Queen's Counsel in 1949. During the Second
World War, he assisted the UK Foreign Office in encouraging Anglo-
American relations. He was a member of the British War Crimes
Executive from 1945–6 and attended the Nuremberg trials. He
became a member of the Institute of International Law in 1947, a
fellow of the British Academy in 1948 and a member of the United
Nations International Law Commission and Judge of the International
Court of Justice in 1951. Lauterpacht authored several publications
and was an acknowledged authority on international law. He was
knighted in 1956. In his youth Lauterpacht helped to establish the
World Federation of Jewish Students. He supported the Hebrew
University of Jerusalem and many Jewish charities. The loss of his
family in the Holocaust made Lauterpacht's fight for human rights
even more essential.

Harold Lever

Cabinet Minister and economic
adviser to Labour prime ministers
1914–1995

Harold Lever was born in
Cheetham, Manchester. His
parents, Bernard and Bertha
Lever, were Orthodox Jews
who had emigrated from
Lithuania. Lever was educated
at Manchester Grammar School and Manchester University, where
he studied law. He was called to the bar aged 21, and practised on
the north-western circuit from 1935–1939. In 1945, he abandoned
law to stand as MP for the Exchange Division of Manchester, and he
would hold a seat in the House of Commons until 1979, when he
was named a life peer and joined the House of Lords. His superior
knowledge of financial markets led Harold Wilson and James
Callaghan to rely on him for advice at times of economic crisis. He
became a member of the cabinet in 1969 as Paymaster-General and
deputy to Tony Benn at the Ministry of Technology, and helped the
Wilson government negotiate key aspects of international agreements
that saved Britain from a currency crisis in 1968. When Labour were
defeated in the 1970 general election, Lever became Chairman of the
Public Accounts Committee. On Labour's return to power in 1974, he
became Chancellor of the Duchy of Lancaster (1974–9).

Solomon Lever

Union leader and
Mayor of Hackney
1895-1959

Solomon Lever was the son of
Jewish immigrants from Bialystok
in modern day Poland. His father,
Nathan, was a cabinet maker in
Bethnal Green. Lever attended
the Jews Free School, before
following his father's career. As Solomon Levetsky, he served with
the Royal Flying Corps during the First World War as a mechanic. An
active trade unionist and member of the East End Worker's Circle,
Lever later became General Secretary of the London Jewish Baker's
Union. He served as a labour councillor for Hackney from 1945, and
was a well-known supporter of Zionism and prominent anti-fascist
campaigner. In 1951, he was elected Mayor of Hackney. In 1959
Lever was abducted by thieves posing as police detectives to gain
access to the funds of the Worker's Circle Friendly Society which
Lever managed. He died of a heart attack during the ordeal and his
body was found dumped on a road in Epping Forest. No one was ever
charged in connection with the crime. A popular figure, Lever was
known as "Uncle Solly" within the Jewish East End community.

Leone Levi
Barrister and statistician
1821–1888

Leone Levi was born in Ancona, Italy to an orthodox Jewish family. His education at school was poor and he left at 14 to go into commerce. He came to Liverpool, England in 1844 to expand his brother's business and was naturalised in 1847. Levi advocated the creation of a chamber of commerce and became Honorary Secretary upon its establishment in 1849. He went on to write *Commercial Law: Its Principles and Administration* (1851), which received national and international acclaim. In 1852 Levi was appointed Professor of the Principles and Practice of Commerce and Commercial Law at King's College, London and he advocated the need for civil judicial statistics, which were later released annually. In 1854 Levi's work led to the Mercantile Law Amendment Act. His proposals to reform the law of arbitration led to clauses in the Common-Law Procedure Act (1854). Levi became a barrister in 1859 and was an office-holder in many societies, including the Royal Statistical Society and the Royal Geographic Society. His best-known work, *History of British Commerce*, was published in 1872. On settling in England, Leone converted to Christianity and joined the Presbyterian Church. He was awarded the Order of the Crown of Italy.

Barnett Lewis
Decorated hero of
the London Blitz
1900–1979

Barnett "Barney" Lewis was born
in the East End of London, to
Lewis Karbatchnick and his wife
Chaya née Glickenhouse, who
were both émigrés from eastern
Europe. He was one of two
brothers and six sisters. Barney later changed his surname to Lewis,
his father's forename. At the outbreak of the Second World War he
joined the Air Raid Precaution (ARP) Service. While off-duty during
a night-time air raid on 23 September 1940, he heard that a pub
in East Ham had been bombed, and thinking it might be the one in
which he lived with his sister and brother-in-law, he joined the rescue
party. Several men were trapped in public air raid shelters whose roofs
had collapsed, and which were now flooding from a burst water main.
Lewis helped to free a man pinned underneath the collapsed roof
by jacking up the rubble through sheer strength and then sawing
through timbers, rescuing him just as the water had reached his head.
He was one of two men awarded the George Medal for saving lives
that night under difficult and dangerous conditions.

George Henry Lewis

Leading lawyer of the
Victorian era
1833–1911

George Henry Lewis was born
in Holborn, London. He was
one of eight children of James
Graham Lewis, founder of the
successful law firm Lewis & Lewis,
and Harriet Davis. Lewis was
educated at a private Jewish school in Edmonton and at University
College School, London and was subsequently taken into partnership
by his father and uncle. He achieved notoriety for his role in the
inquest into the poisoning of Charles Bravo (1876) and from then
on became attached to the most notorious criminal causes célèbres
of the period. Lewis became one of the most sought-after solicitors
of his day, and at the request of Oscar Wilde represented Wilde's
blackmailed friend Lord Alfred Douglas. He was selected by the
Parnell Commission to conduct the case for Charles Stewart Parnell
and the Irish Parliamentary Party against *The Times*, for which he
was rewarded with a knighthood in 1892. He received a baronetcy
in the 1902 Coronation Honours List and was made CVO in 1905.
He contributed to the movement that led to the Moneylenders
Act (1900), which required registration for moneylenders, and his
testimony to the Royal Commission on the divorce laws (1910)
brought forth equal rights for both sexes and cheaper divorce.

Harold Lightman

Barrister

1906–1998

Harold Lightman was born in Leeds. His father had emigrated from Lithuania and his mother was Scottish-born with German parentage. He was educated at the City of Leeds School and left at 14 to enter his father's furniture business. He studied at evening classes and qualified as an accountant. He joined the Liberal Party but chose not to stand for parliament, despite being offered three seats, qualifying instead as a barrister in 1932. Lightman started at a disadvantage due to antisemitism and his lack of university education. However, his knowledge of accountancy proved useful and he was especially called upon for cases involving company law and insolvency. He became a Queen's Counsel in 1955 and Head of Chambers in 1966. His career was cut short in 1967 when he suffered a stroke. Lightman was active in the Jewish community, serving as President of the Central Synagogue Orphan Aid Society and in the Anglo-Jewish Association. He was a member of the West London Synagogue.

Manasseh Masseh Lopes
Tory politician
1755–1831

Manasseh Masseh Lopes was born in Jamaica, the only son of Mordecai Rodriguez Lopes, a plantation owner, and his wife Rebecca. Both were Sephardi Jews who had emigrated from Portugal to Jamaica and made their wealth as sugar planters. Lopes inherited a substantial fortune in 1796 upon the death of his father, who had by then settled in Clapham, and Lopes spent £100,000 buying the Heywood estates in Devon in 1798. By 1820, he had become one of the largest landowners in Devon. In 1802, Lopes converted to Christianity and was baptised in the Church of England. That same year, he bought his first seat in parliament as Tory member for New Romney, Kent. He became a firm supporter of William Pitt and for his loyalty was created a baronet in 1805, one of the first persons of Jewish descent to be given a hereditary title. In 1810, he purchased the borough of Westbury with the intention of ensuring his electoral success, and was appointed High Sheriff of Devon. In 1819, however, Lopes was discovered to have bribed the voters in the previous year's general election, and was subsequently fined and jailed for two years. On his release from prison, Lopes continued in public life and was returned in 1823 unopposed for Westbury.

Gertrude Lowy
Suffragette
1887–1982

Gertrude Lowy was the daughter of wealthy stockbroker Ernest Lowy and his wife Henrietta. The whole family helped to support and finance the Women's Social and Political Union (WSPU), which was the more radical suffrage union, set up and run by Emmeline Pankhurst in 1903. Their slogan was "Deeds, not words". In March 1912, Gertrude was sentenced to two months' hard labour for having taken part in a WSPU window-smashing raid. Her mother and sisters, Ethel and Lina, were also militant activists and her younger sister Ruth took part in a deputation to Buckingham Palace on 21 May 1914. Gertrude was awarded a Hunger Strike medal for valour by the WSPU, which indicated that she had served a prison sentence for militancy and been subjected to the painful procedure of force-feeding, which often led to ill-health.

Henrietta Lowy
Suffragette
1866–1953

Henrietta Lowy, neé Solomon, was married to Ernest Lowy and the whole family were involved in the fight for women's rights. After hearing Mrs Pankhurst speak at a meeting at the Paddington Baths, Henrietta joined the Women's Social and Political Union (WSPU) together with one of her daughters. Two suffrage plays were performed in the drawing room of her Holland Park house for the entertainment of the Kensington WSPU. Both Henrietta and her husband made generous donations to the WSPU fund. In 1910, she was sentenced to one month's imprisonment for taking part in the stone-throwing retaliation for "Black Friday" and was convicted again in 1912 for breaking a window during the demonstrations in March that year. Henrietta was a tax resister and joined the Jewish League for Woman Suffrage when it was founded in 1912. She was a supporter of the East London Federation of Suffragettes, which was led by Sylvia Pankhurst. Four of her daughters were actively involved in the WSPU and her son Albert was a member of the Men's Political Union.

Helen Lucas
Philanthropist
1835–1918

Helen Lucas was the eldest of nine children of Frederick Goldsmid and his wife Caroline Samuel. Her religious education began early, with her father teaching her Hebrew at the age of six. She married merchant Lionel Lucas in 1855 and had two children. After her husband died in 1862, Lucas devoted her life and much of her wealth to philanthropy. From 1880 she was President of the Ladies' Conjoint Visiting Committee of the Jewish Board of Guardians and president of its workrooms from 1896, where girls learned skills including needlework and embroidery. She gave religious instruction during her weekly visits and set a high standard with regard to cleanliness and punctuality. Her generosity to the poor extended to both Jews and Christians and she had traditional views on family life. She commented on communal affairs regularly in the Jewish press. Lucas was involved with the National Union of Women Workers and the Union of Jewish Women. She was an active member of the West London Reform Synagogue, seeking to prevent change to the liturgy, and was actively interested in education and health, supporting many charities, including the Jewish Religious Education Board.

Fritz A. Mann
Academic lawyer
1907–1991

Frederick Alexander Mann was born in Frankenthal, Germany, to father Richard, a lawyer, and mother, Ida, née Oppenheim. Both parents were Jewish. Mann studied at the Universities of Geneva, Munich and Berlin. In 1930, Mann became an assistant in the Berlin law faculty, a rare honour. He took his doctorate in 1931. Fleeing the Nazis in 1933, Mann settled in England, working as a consultant in German law. Mann's thesis, *The Legal Aspect of Money*, was published in 1938. It was the first study of the law of money in English. In 1946, Mann was naturalised, and began practising as a solicitor and also worked with the Allied Control Commission to eradicate Nazi laws in Germany. In 1960 he was appointed Visiting Professor at the University of Bonn. In 1973, Mann published *Studies in International Law* and was made a British Fellow in 1974. Mann was awarded Germany's Grand Cross of the Order of Merit in 1977 and the British CBE in 1980. In the last year of his life, Mann was elected an honorary Bencher of Gray's Inn and became the first practising solicitor to be an honorary Queen's Counsel.

Alan Marre

Health service commissioner

1914–1990

Alan Marre was born Alan Moshinsky in Bow, east London. His parents were Russian Jews who had settled in England in 1907. Marre, along with his elder brother, anglicised his surname in 1941. He was educated at St Olave's and St Saviour's Grammar School, Southwark, and Trinity Hall, Cambridge. Marre entered the Ministry of Health in 1936, as an assistant principal, and helped to launch the National Health Service. He became a principal in 1941, Assistant Secretary in 1946 and Undersecretary in 1952. In 1963, he briefly moved to the Ministry of Labour, but returned to the Ministry of Health as Deputy Secretary in 1964. In 1971 Marre became Britain's second parliamentary and health service ombudsman, and investigated complaints of maladministration by government departments. In 1973 he became the first Health Service Commissioner, and carried out a similar role for the NHS. From 1979–85, he was Vice-Chairman of the advisory committee on distinction awards for NHS consultants. He was knighted in 1970. Although Marre was not a practising Jew, he devoted much of his time to Jewish causes and became the President of the Maccabaeans in 1982.

Eleanor Marx
Socialist writer and activist
1855–1898

Jenny Julia Eleanor Marx was born in Soho, London, the sixth child of Karl Marx and his wife Jenny. She was educated at South Hampstead College for Ladies, leaving at 14. Life in the Marx home contributed hugely to her education in literature and politics and in 1869 she travelled to Ireland with her father's collaborator Friedrich Engels, and was a supporter of the Fenian cause. In 1871, news of the Paris Commune and its violent suppression began her political activism and she organised aid for French refugees in London. Her parents' ill-health meant she spent much of her time caring for them, while working as her father's researcher and secretary. After his death in 1883, she was free to pursue her own political career and began to live openly with Edward Aveling, a married zoologist. She published a pamphlet on socialist feminism, co-written with Aveling, entitled *The Woman Question* (1886), and produced the first English translation of Flaubert's *Madame Bovary*. From 1889, Eleanor campaigned for and with workers, leading the British dockworkers' and gas workers' trades unions and defending Jewish workers. She was the only member of the Marx family to claim her Jewishness.

Anthony Meyer
Conservative politician
1920–2004

Anthony Meyer was born in London to Sir Frank Meyer, a businessman and politician, and his wife Georgina. Anthony's grandfather, Sir Carl Meyer, had come from Hamburg and made his fortune with the Rothschild bank. Anthony served as a lieutenant in the Scots Guards during the Second World War. After being wounded by shrapnel he met his future wife Barbadee, who nursed him back to health. In the early 1950s Meyer worked at the Paris Embassy and within the Foreign Office. In 1964 he was elected Conservative MP for Eton and Slough. However, he lost his seat two years later. In parliament, Meyer spoke in favour of abolishing the death penalty and enthusiastically supported a close alliance with Europe. In 1970 he became MP for West Flintshire and was appointed Employment Secretary two years later. He opposed the 1982 Falklands War and became increasingly critical of Margaret Thatcher. In 1989 he famously challenged Thatcher for the Tory leadership. Although he was unsuccessful and widely criticised, he said he made "the unthinkable thinkable". His challenge indirectly contributed to the end of an era when Thatcher stood down in 1990.

Ian Mikardo
Politician
1908–1993

Ian Mikardo was born in Portsmouth, the son of Moshe Mikardo, a tailor from Poland, and his wife Bluma, from Ukraine. They had settled in the East End around 1900, but later lived in Portsmouth, where Moshe worked as a tailor for the Royal Navy. Ian Mikardo was educated at Portsmouth Grammar School and worked as a management consultant and for the Supervisory Staffs Association. He was elected Labour MP for Reading in 1945 and served as an MP from 1945–59 and 1964–87. He never held ministerial office but was Chairman of the House of Commons Select Committee on Nationalised Industries and was also Chairman of the Labour Party in 1970–71. Always on the left of the party, he was a leading member of the "Keep Left" and "Victory for Socialism" groups, alongside other extreme left-wing Labour figures. Mikardo also established close business relations with the Soviet Union and the eastern bloc countries, and was widely viewed as a "fellow traveller." Always an ardent Zionist, he was close to left-wing Israeli parties like Mapam. Incongruously, he was regarded by all sides of politics as the House of Commons' bookmaker, and wrote a book on gambling.

Ralph Miliband
Internationally renowned
Marxist thinker
1924–1994

Ralph Miliband was born in
Brussels. His parents were Jewish
immigrants from Poland. Miliband
was a member of Hashomer
Hatzair, a socialist-Zionist
group for young people. He
and his father left Poland for Britain in 1940 to escape the Germans.
Miliband knew little English but, after a short employment in the Blitz
clean-up operations, received a refugee grant enabling him to attend
the LSE. Miliband published his first book in 1961, a Marxist criticism
of the Labour Party entitled *Parliamentary Socialism*, in which he
argued the party had failed to enact truly radical change in its history
because it had prioritised constitutionalism over socialism. The book
established him as a prominent figure on the left, and Miliband saw
it as his duty to revitalise the movement. He established the *Socialist
Register* in 1964 with this in mind, bringing together the world's
leading Marxist thinkers. Miliband published a number of major
works over the next 30 years, including *Marxism and Politics* (1977),
Capitalist Democracy in Britain (1982) and his final book *Socialism for
a Sceptical Age* (1994), which addressed the threat of neoliberalism.
Miliband's two sons, David and Edward, became leading figures in the
Labour Party.

Victor Mishcon
Solicitor and politician
1915–2006

Victor Mishcon was born in Brixton, London. His father, a rabbi, had emigrated from Poland. Mishcon was educated at the City of London School and became a solicitor, establishing his own practice in Brixton in 1936 and in central London in the late 1950s. In 1988, his firm merged to become Mishcon de Reya. Among Victor's best-known clients were Ruth Ellis (the last woman to be hanged in England), Donald Campbell, Jeffrey Archer and Princess Diana. From 1955 Mishcon held positions as a Labour county councillor on the Lambeth, London and Greater London Councils. In 1978 he was made a life peer as Baron Mishcon of Lambeth and served as Opposition Labour Home Affairs Spokesman in the House of Lords from 1983– 1990 and Shadow Lord Chancellor from 1990–1992. In 1992 he became one of the first solicitors to be appointed an Honorary Queen's Counsel. Mishcon was active in Jewish and Israeli affairs. He was President of the Association of Jewish Youth, Vice-President of the Board of Deputies, Chairman of the Institute of Jewish Studies, Governor of Technion, Israel and Vice-Chairman of the Council of Christians and Jews. He was awarded the Star of Jordan by King Hussein for acting as a secret intermediary in negotiations between Jordan and Israel during the 1980s.

Alan Mocatta
Judge
1907–1990

Alan Mocatta was born in Paddington, London, to a long-established Jewish family who had arrived in England in 1671. He was educated at Polack's House, Clifton College and New College, Oxford. In 1930 he became a barrister. During the Second World War, he served as an officer with the War Office and was awarded the Order of the British Empire in 1944. After the war, he developed an extensive commercial practice and became a Queen's Counsel in 1951. In 1961 he was appointed as a judge of the high court of justice, Queen's bench division and was knighted. In 1970 he became President of the Restrictive Practices Court. Mocatta was very active in the Jewish community. He was President of the Spanish and Portuguese Congregation, Chairman of Jews' College Council, president of the Sephardi Home for the Aged and a member of the Anglo-Jewish Association. He was also President of the Jewish Historical Society and Chairman of the appeal for a new synagogue and Jewish centre in Oxford. He was a keen cricketer, often playing for the village team in the small Cornish village where he had a country house.

Frederic David Mocatta

Philanthropist and promoter
of Jewish religion and culture
1828–1905

Frederic David Mocatta was
born in London to Anglo-Jewish
banker Abraham Mocatta and his
wife Miriam Brandon. Educated
at home by private tutors, he
was also taught Hebrew and
Latin by his father. He entered the family firm of Mocatta & Goldsmid,
bullion brokers to the Bank of England, in 1843, retiring in 1874. He
married Mary Ada Goldsmid in 1856. Mocatta devoted his energies
to numerous charitable causes. Education and the condition of the
working classes of all creeds concerned him but he wanted to make
the poor independent of charity. He supported many voluntary
hospitals and a great deal of his wealth went to Jewish charities.
Mocatta was a member of the Jewish Board of Guardians, and was
deeply concerned with the plight of persecuted Jews under Russian
rule. However, he wished to discourage large numbers of them
from settling in Britain and attempted to suppress the spread of
socialism among the Russian-Jewish working class in London. His
library, bequeathed to the Mocatta Museum and Library, located
in University College, came to form a foundation for Jewish studies.
The Mocatta Mantle, an ornate Torah mantle commissioned by the
Mocatta family, is now held in the collection of the Jewish Museum,
London.

Edwin Samuel Montagu
Politician
1879–1924

Edwin Samuel Montagu was born in Kensington, the son of Samuel Montagu, 1st Baron Swaythling (1832–1911), millionaire banker, Liberal MP and founder of the Federation of Synagogues. Henrietta Franklin (1866–1964) and Lilian Helen Montagu (1870–1963) were his sisters, and Herbert Samuel (1870–1963) was his cousin. Montagu was educated at Clifton College and the City of London School, and then at University College London and Cambridge, where he was president of the Cambridge Union. He served as a Liberal MP from 1906–22, holding junior appointments to 1915 and then becoming a cabinet minister, most importantly as Secretary of State for India, from 1917–22. As Indian secretary, Montagu was bitterly opposed by many right-wing MPs, their attacks often tinged with antisemitism, for condemning the Amritsar Massacre launched by General Reginald Dyer in 1919, and for Montagu's joint authorship of the Montagu-Chelmsford Report, which recommended the increased participation of native Indians in running the country. He is best remembered today for his hostility to the Balfour Declaration, which he believed was anti-Semitic, and succeeded in modifying the terms. He is also remembered for his marriage to Venetia Stanley, the daughter of Lord Sheffield, who converted to Judaism upon her marriage in order for her husband to retain a legacy from his very Orthodox father. The marriage was unsuccessful, with Venetia having several affairs, including one (preceding her marriage but apparently continuing later) with Prime Minister Herbert Asquith, and another with Lord Beaverbrook.

Lilian Helen Montagu

Established liberal Judaism
in Britain
1873–1963

Lilian Montagu was born
in London. Her father was
the merchant banker and
philanthropist Samuel Montagu.
He raised Lilian in an Orthodox
Jewish tradition and she was
privately educated. At the age of 15, Montagu decided it was her
path to help her fellow Jews. She could not, as a woman, become
a rabbi so devoted herself to social care. In 1899, Montagu wrote
an article for the *Jewish Quarterly Review* criticising the stagnation
of Judaism in Britain and proposing a modern, egalitarian form. She
was drawn to the tenets of liberal Judaism and its proponent, Claude
Montefiore, and eventually persuaded him to lead the newly formed
Jewish Religion Union. While they did not intend to be revolutionary,
their desire to emancipate Jewish women did not sit well with
Jewish leaders, or with Montagu's father. But the JRU grew in size,
acquiring its first minister in 1911 and establishing the Liberal Jewish
Synagogue in Marylebone. By 1944 they had moved to a larger site
in St John's Wood Road and Montagu was ordained as a lay minister.
Despite this religious transformation, Montagu always adhered to the
Orthodox traditions her father had taught her.

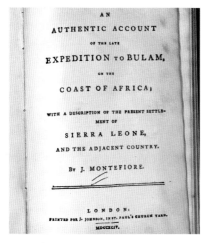

Joshua Montefiore

First Jewish army captain

1762–1843

Joshua Montefiore was born in the City of London, to Jewish parents. He studied law at Oxford University and was admitted to the bar in 1784. He was also a keen adventurer, and in 1791 participated in an expedition to establish a British colony without slave labour off the west coast of Africa, near Sierra Leone. However, he was forced to withdraw after several conflicts with the natives, and documented the encounter in *An Authentic Account of the Late Expedition to Bulam* (1794). On his return to England, he allegedly declined a knighthood and entered the army, becoming the first Jew to hold the rank of captain in the British army. While practising law in London, he achieved considerable success as the author of several useful guides to commercial law, including *Law of Copyright* (1802), *A Commercial Dictionary* (1803), *Traders and Manufacturers Compendium* (1804) and *Commercial and Notarial Precedents* (1804). Around 1810, Montefiore emigrated to the USA, where he retired from law and edited a New York weekly political journal, *Men and Measures*. He was married three times, and raised his eight children as Protestants.

Moses Montefiore

Businessman and supporter
of Jewish rights
1784–1885

Moses Montefiore was born in
Leghorn, Italy, during his parents'
travels. His parents were Italian
Sephardi Jews who had settled in
Kennington, London. Montefiore
was privately educated in
London, after which he briefly worked as a clerk with a firm of tea
merchants. In 1803, he became one of the 12 "Jewish brokers" at
the London stock exchange, and remained a member until 1845,
although his business interests had expanded by then. Montefiore
was a founder of Alliance Assurance (1824), and helped to establish
the Provincial Bank of Ireland (1825), which meant that by 1830, he
was able to retire from business and devote his time solely to Jewish
causes. Montefiore, who had not been a practising Jew, returned
to his Orthodox roots after a visit to the Holy Land in 1827. From
then on, he became strictly observant, and would travel with a
personal shohet (ritual slaughterer) to keep kosher. From 1835–74,
he was president of the London Committee of Deputies of British
Jews, but devoted his time to helping oppressed Jewish communities
abroad. He was knighted by Queen Victoria in 1838, and received a
baronetcy in 1846, in recognition of his services to Jewish people.

Claus Moser

British statistician and
influential public servant
1922–2015

Claus Moser was born in Berlin,
Germany. His father, Ernst Moser,
was the owner of a bank, and
his mother, Lotte, was a talented
musician. The family moved to
England in 1936 and Moser
attended Frensham Heights School, Surrey, and the London School of
Economics. In 1940, he was interned at Huyton Camp, Liverpool as
a "friendly enemy alien", along with other Jewish refugees, and it was
here that he discovered an interest in statistics. He became a lecturer
in statistics at the London School of Economics in 1943, and worked
his way up to become Reader in 1955, and Professor of Social
Statistics from 1961–70. In 1967 Moser was appointed Director of
the Central Statistical Office by Harold Wilson, where he remained
for 11 years. A firm believer in the importance of education, he was
Warden of Wadham College, Oxford (1984–93), Chancellor of Keele
University (1986–2002), President of the British Association for
the Advancement of Science (1989–90) and Pro-Vice-Chancellor of
Oxford University (1991–3). In 1997, a dedicated research facility
for the humanities and social sciences was established at Keele
University in his name. Music was Moser's greatest passion, and he
was Chairman of the Royal Opera House from 1974–87, in addition
to serving on the governing body of the Royal Academy of Music.
In 2001 he was made a life peer with the title Baron Moser. He also
served on the Board of the Jewish Museum London.

Sara Moshkowitz

First Jewish woman to be called
to the bar in England
fl. 1920–1950

Sara Moshkowitz was born
in Kishinev, Moldova and
migrated to Britain in 1920.
Following three years of tireless
preparatory law study, she
was accepted by Lincoln's Inn.
Graduating near the top of her class in her final law examinations,
Moshkowitz became the first Jewish woman to be called to the bar in
England in 1925. Her speciality was commercial law. Outside of her
work, Moshkowitz's passion was painting. She exhibited at the Royal
Academy in 1930, and was commissioned to paint the portrait of
the well-known London magistrate J.A.R. Cairns. She also regularly
addressed meetings of Zionist societies in England. In her later years,
Moshkowitz left England for Israel and practised at the Israeli bar,
under her married surname Moshkowitz-Varkonyi.

Edith Munro

Volunteer nurse who died
on active service
1894–1916

The daughter of a Scottish
father and Jewish mother, Edith
Munro was born in Poplar, east
London and raised in nearby
Hackney. She started nursing
at the Albert Dock Seaman's
Hospital in Silvertown, east London. In 1914 she joined the Voluntary
Aid Detachment (VAD), a volunteer nurses group formed in 1909
to serve in war zones with British and Imperial armed forces. In 1916
she contracted acute bronchopneumonia while on duty and died of
heart failure aged 23. She was buried privately the following day in
Plashet Jewish Cemetery in East Ham, London, her grave remaining
unrecognised until she received a Commonwealth War Graves
headstone in 1914. To mark the centenary of her death in 2016 a
stone-setting ceremony was held and wreaths were laid at her grave
in a special service held on International Women's Day, led by HM
Armed Forces Chaplain Rabbi Major Reuben Livingstone and attended
by members of her family and dignitaries.

Derrick Nabarro
Great Escapist
1921–1992

Derrick David William Nabarro was born in Edmonton, London, to father Joel and mother Ethel, née Dearden. During the Second World War Nabarro enlisted in the RAF. In 1941 his plane was shot down during a bombing raid over Bremen. He was captured and interned at Stalag IXC, Bad Sulsa. Nabarro attempted to escape twice before simply walking out the front gate without being stopped. Fleeing across Europe, he was caught again but escaped overnight from the police station where he was being held. Travelling through Belgium, Nabarro reached France, was captured again but pretended to be escaping the Allies in Paris, so his captors escorted him to French Vichy. Faced with being taken back to Paris, Nabarro revealed that he was an Ally, and was interned in Fort de la Rivere, Monte Carlo, in March 1942. Nabarro became one of the masterminds behind a large-scale escape, in August 1942, from the POW camp and was among 32 men to reach safety in England. In 1943 Nabarro was awarded the Distinguished Conduct Medal and wrote *Wait for the Dawn* in 1952, an account of his escapes.

Harry Louis Nathan
Liberal politician who later
joined the Labour Party
1889–1963

Harry Louis Nathan was born in
London, the son of a fine arts
publisher, and was educated at
St Paul's School, where he served
in the school's cadet corps
alongside his classmate, the
future Field Marshal Bernard Montgomery. Nathan became a solicitor
in London, specialising in commercial law, and acted as legal advisor
to the British Zionist Federation. He was also closely associated with
the Palestine Potash Corporation and other Zionist causes. Nathan
was a Liberal MP from 1929–34, when he joined the Labour Party,
but was defeated at the 1935 general election. He was then elected a
Labour MP in 1937, serving until 1940, when he was given a peerage
as 1st Baron Nathan, and held office as Undersecretary for War
and Vice-President of the Army Council in 1945–6, and as Minister
of Civil Aviation in 1946–8. He later became head of the Wolfson
Foundation. His wife Eleanor née Stettauer (1892–1972) was
Chairman of the London County Council in 1947–8, and Chairman
of the West London Synagogue.

Matthew Nathan
Civil servant and
colonial governor
1862–1939

Matthew Nathan was born in
Paddington, the son of Jonah
Nathan, a manufacturing
stationer, and Miriam née
Jacobs. He was educated by
private tutors and at the Royal
Military Academy at Woolwich, where he graduated first in his class.
He was promoted to captain and, in 1898, to major, and, from the
mid-1890s, began an extraordinary upward ascent. In 1895 Nathan
became Secretary to the Colonial Defence Committee and, in 1900,
was appointed Governor of the Gold Coast. He served until 1904
when he was made Governor of Hong Kong, serving until 1909.
His ascendancy continued: Secretary to the General Post Office
(1909–11), Chairman of the Board of the Inland Revenue (1911–14)
and, in 1914, Permanent Undersecretary for Ireland. During his tenure
in Ireland the disastrous Dublin Easter Uprising of 1916 forced his
resignation. Nathan then became Permanent Undersecretary of
pensions (1916–19), and then Governor of Queensland (1920–25),
where he did much to preserve the Great Barrier Reef. He also served
as High Sheriff of Somerset in 1934–35. Nathan was knighted in
1902, and two of his brothers also became knights: Sir Frederick
Lewis Nathan (1861–1933), President of the Institution of Chemical
Engineers, 1925–27; and Sir Robert Nathan (1867–1921), Secretary
to the Indian Universities Committee, 1902–10.

Harold Newgass
George Cross winner
1899–1984

Harold Reginald Newgass was born in London. He joined the Territorial Army in 1918, serving for 16 years in the Royal Artillery. In 1940, Newgass joined the Royal Naval Volunteer Reserve, serving in Liverpool. During a German bombing raid, a parachute mine landed in Garston Gas Works but failed to explode, resting nose-down and upright. It was the size of a tugboat funnel. Because of the gas supply to the factory, the potential explosion would be devastating. 6,000 people were evacuated from the area and Newgass climbed down to inspect the bomb in what would be described as one of the most hazardous bomb disposal assignments ever undertaken. Newgass was forced to use a breathing cylinder, with only 30 minutes of oxygen supply, and got through six of them over the course of his two-day defusing mission. Single-handedly Newgass surrounded the bomb with sandbags and removed the fuse, primer and detonator before rendering the device inert by removing the clock mechanism. In 1941, Temporary Lieutenant Newgass received the George Cross. The medal, along with his Defence Medal and War Medal 1939–45, are displayed in London's Imperial War Museum.

Isidore Newman
SOE hero
1916–1944

Isidore Newman was born in Leeds. His Lithuanian-Jewish parents, Joseph Naviprutsky and Tilly née Cohen, were both tailors. Educated in Durham, Newman trained as a teacher. In 1940 he joined the Royal Corps of Signals, stationed in Sheffield. In 1941 Newman was selected for Special Operation's Executive F-Section and trained as a radio operative. It was noted during his training that his French wasn't particularly good. Despite this Newman worked on Operation Divided in occupied France and was promoted to captain. Newman also served under the guise of "Jacques Nemorin" on the "Urchin" circuit of wireless operators on the Cote d'Azur. In 1943, Newman joined the "Salesman" circuit of clandestine radio operatives, sending vital messages and information from behind enemy lines. In 1944, Newman was captured by the Gestapo along with almost 80 members of the "Salesman" circuit. Sent to Mauthausen concentration camp in September 1944, Newman was shot along with other F-Section operatives. He was posthumously awarded the MBE in 1946 "for his courage and devotion to duty".

Opposite Cryptologists Max Newman and Rolf Noskwith used this Second World War Bombe machine to help decipher German Enigma messages

"The geese that laid
the golden eggs and
never cackled."

Winston Churchill's description of the code breakers at Bletchley Park

Max Newman
Bletchley Park hero
1897–1984

Maxwell Herman Alexander Neumann was born in Chelsea, London, to Herman Alexander Neumann, a German secretary, and Sarah, née Pike, a schoolteacher. Neumann studied at City of London School and St John's College, Cambridge. He changed his surname to Newman in 1916. Newman became a St John's fellow in 1923 and lecturer in 1927. A pioneer of combinatory topology, Newman wrote several significant papers and a 1939 book, *Elements of the Topology of Plane Sets of Points*. In 1942 he enlisted at the government code and cypher school at Bletchley Park and familiarised himself with the German Tunny cipher system, a superior teleprinter to Enigma. Along with Alan Turing, Newman pushed through the building of Colossus, a code-breaking computer for the Allies and the world's first large-scale electronic computer. The section where it was housed was named The Newmanry after him. After the war Newman became the Fieldon Professor of Maths at Manchester until his retirement, pushing his belief that general-purpose computers would become widespread. In 1959 Newman was awarded the Sylvester Medal of the Royal Society and in 1962 the De Morgan Medal of the London Mathematical Society.

Rolf Noskwith

Codebreaker

1919–2017

Rolf Noskovitch was born in Chemnitz, Germany to Jewish parents. His father was Chaim, who owned a clothing factory, and his mother was Malka, née Ginsberg. For business reasons the family moved to Britain in 1932, changed their surname and set up Charnos, a textiles firm, in Derbyshire. Noskwith went to Nottingham High School and studied maths at Trinity College, Cambridge. It was here, in 1941, that his potential talent for codebreaking was spotted. Previously he had been rejected by the British army because of his German heritage, but Noskwith was accepted to Bletchley Park as a translator and cryptographer. The success of Bletchley's codebreaking led the Germans to introduce the Enigma machine in 1942. It took Noskwith and the team almost a year to crack the coding, but once they had, the German navy's effectiveness was greatly damaged. Noskwith continued working on Engima until 1945. His greatest achievement was codebreaking the Naval Enigma Offizier settings, permitting the Allies to read messages between Kriegsmarine officers. After the war, Noskwith moved to GCHQ, Bletchley Park's successor, deciphering a backlog of Japanese naval messages and Yugoslavian codes. In 1946 he started working for Charnos, becoming chairman in 1957.

"It was the bell of the great Ghetto school, summoning its pupils from the reeking courts and alleys…"

Israel Zangwill, *Children of The Ghetto*, 1892, student and teacher at the Jews' Free School

Jewish Philanthropy and Philanthropists

The Jews' Free School was established at Bell Lane, Spitalfields, London, 1817, to provide basic education to the poor Jewish community in London's East End.

The workroom at St James's workhouse, from *The Microcosm of London*, 1808

Jewish Philanthropy and Philanthropists

Professor William D. Rubinstein
Historian and Author

Jews have always been known for their generosity in funding philanthropic ventures and institutions, regarding tzedakah (charity) as a moral obligation. While most Jewish philanthropy has been directed at the poorer, less fortunate or persecuted members of the Jewish community, in recent years many wealthy Jews have also contributed to funding important educational, medical and charitable activities for the whole community. In 19th-century Britain, a small elite of wealthy Jews found themselves in a community with many impoverished Jews, often recent immigrants from eastern Europe, and responded with generosity. It is fair to say that the aim of most Jewish charitable activities aimed at less fortunate Jews has been, wherever possible, to help these Jews rise up the social scale, rather than remain indefinitely as welfare recipients.

In 19th-century Britain, there was no welfare state in the modern sense. There were no state pensions, unemployment insurance or a free health service, and the state did not provide housing or jobs. From the 1830s, the only publicly funded form of aid to the unemployed or elderly was the workhouse, which could be found in most parishes in the country. Anyone could enter a workhouse (the sexes were separated), where they were given a bed and basic meals. For many Jews, and apart from the contempt for the poor this system strongly implied, there were difficulties specific to them, for instance the (non-) provision of kosher food and the (non-) recognition of the Jewish Sabbath, with Anglican clergymen

185

regularly present. Many Jews were also concerned at Christian conversionist missionaries who operated in heavily Jewish areas, often offering food and lodging in exchange for baptism.

In 1859, the leaders of the three main Ashkenazi synagogues in London, determined to provide a better system of charitable relief for London's needy Jews, formed the Jewish Board of Guardians. This body has continued to exist since then, changing its name to the Jewish Welfare Board in 1963 and to Jewishcare in 1990, after it merged with the Jewish Blind Society and other Jewish charities. Its early officers and trustees read like a "Who's Who" of the major "Jewish Cousinhood" families, often wealthy businessmen in the City of London, and often intermarried. The two major early leaders of the Jewish Board of Guardians were Ephraim Alex (1800–82; President of the Board from 1859 to 1869) and Lionel Louis Cohen (1832–8; president from 1869 until 1887). Alex did not come from a wealthy background, but was a dentist who had been overseer of the Great Synagogue in London. Cohen, in contrast, was a wealthy stockbroker and a Conservative MP from 1885 until his premature death, who was related by marriage to the Rothschilds and Montefiores. He was also one of the founders of the "United Synagogue" (the title given to the three city synagogues: the Great, the Hambro and the New). Cohen was succeeded by his brother Sir Benjamin Louis Cohen, 1st Baronet (1844–1909; president 1887–1900), also a stockbroker and a Conservative MP, and then by his son Sir Leonard Lionel Cohen, 2nd Baronet (1858–1938; president 1900–20). Many of the other great "Jewish Cousinhood" families were in evidence as senior figures of the Board of Guardians, including Baron Ferdinand de Rothschild (1831–98) and Nathan Mayer Rothschild, 1st Baron Rothschild (1840–1915, the first professing Jew to receive a peerage), both of whom served as treasurers of the Board of Guardians. The Rothschild family has been notable as philanthropists since then.

The Board of Guardians provided loans, food, clothing and housing to needy Jews, as well as apprenticeships for young men and domestic training for young women. It is believed that about 90 per cent of aid recipients were recent immigrants, while the Board increasingly facilitated the re-emigration of Jews elsewhere, especially to America. Several aspects of its standard policies before the First World War have been controversial: they have been viewed as opposing the mass Jewish immigration from eastern Europe to the East End of London, fearing this would stir up antisemitism, and in being intrusive and officious in distributing charity, although of course the alternative was even worse. The Board also maintained a policy of not giving aid to anyone in Britain for less than six months, fearing that this would lead to a flood of impoverished Jews from Russia who came specifically for the Board's largesse. The Board of Guardians – among other Jewish charitable bodies in England at the time – was also notable for using the talents of women who, like the men, were often drawn from the same wealthy families and who often had a good deal of time on their hands. Among the most notable (of many) were Louisa de Rothschild (née Montefiore, 1821–1910), a friend of Thackeray and Disraeli, who was manager of the Jews' Free School and a founder of the Jewish Association for the Protection of Girls and Women; Hannah Floretta Cohen (1875–1946), the daughter of Sir Benjamin, who in 1900 became the first woman elected to the executive of the Board of Guardians, and served as its president from 1930; and Helen Lucas (née Goldsmid, 1835–1918), President of the Ladies' Committee of the Board of Guardians from 1880 until her death.

Statue of William Shakespeare in Leicester Square bearing an inscription recording the gift of the square to the public by Albert Grant, 1874

Museum of Docklands, now Museum of London Docklands founded by Clive Bourne in 1996

Many early Jewish philanthropists were active in both Jewish and non-Jewish charities. A notable example was Frederick David Mocatta (1828–1905), of another leading "Cousinhood" family, who was a major figure in the Board of Guardians and other Jewish charities, as well as being a leading figure in the RSPCA and in the Charity Organisation Society, which assisted all charities. He was also responsible for the Anglo-Jewish Historical Exhibition of 1887, the first to make the achievements of the Jews in England known to the public. Inevitably, too, some Jewish philanthropists were corrupt as businessmen, a notable example being Baron (of Portugal) Albert Grant (né Gottheimer), a major fraudster – he is believed to be the original of Melmotte in Anthony Trollope's *The Way We Live Now* – who nevertheless in 1873 purchased the site of Leicester Square, then derelict, beautified it and donated it as a public park.

From the late 19th century, there was a general broadening of the range of charities and bequests to which wealthy Jews contributed, beyond aiding the Jewish community alone. Samuel Lewis (1838–1901), who began as a pedlar of cheap jewellery in Birmingham, became probably the most successful moneylender in Britain, but one who was highly regarded by his aristocratic clients, who were normally charged less than at a bank. With his wife, Ada Lewis (née Hill, 1844–1906), he donated £3.4m – an astronomical sum – to 51 charities, especially for working-class housing, such as the Samuel Lewis Houses in central London. Alfred Beit (1853–1906), who, together with his non-Jewish business partner Sir Julius Wernher, took over DeBeers Consolidated, the South African diamond monopoly upon the death of Cecil Rhodes and was very wealthy, moved to London, where he was one of the founders of Imperial College, the great science university in the capital, and also funded the Beit Chair of Colonial History at Oxford. Joseph Joel

Duveen, 1st Baron Duveen (1869–1939), the famous art dealer who sold masterpieces owned by impoverished European aristocrats to American millionaires, donated the hall at the National Gallery in London that houses the Elgin Marbles, which he controversially had steam-cleaned. He also gave galleries and works of art to the Tate and other museums. Because of a perceived conflict of interest as an art dealer, he was forced to resign as a trustee of the National Gallery in 1936. Bernhard Baron (1850–1929) earned a fortune of about £7m (probably £500m today) by inventing a machine to make cigarettes and was the chairman of Carrera's, a major tobacco company and gave away £2m to charity, including funds for the St. George's Settlement House in the East End and £575,000 for children's hospitals. Israel Moses Sieff, Baron Sieff (1889–1972) and his brother-in-law Simon Marks, 1st Baron Marks (1888–1964), the proprietors of Marks & Spencer, were probably the largest contributors to Zionist causes in the world, both during the Mandate period and after the foundation of the State of Israel. They were particularly close to Chaim Weizmann, later the first president of Israel, when they all lived in Manchester. Sieff's son Marcus Joseph Sieff, Baron Sieff of Brimpton (1913–2001), was President of the United Joint Jewish Appeal in Britain, and also a contributor to many other charities.

During the post-1945 period, Jewish philanthropy, if anything, became more generous and also more visible, as wealthy Jews attached their names to many projects benefiting the wider community. Among the best-known Jewish philanthropists of the post-1945 period was Sir Isaac Wolfson, 1st Baronet (1897–1991), who made a fortune in the mail-order business and as a retailer. In 1955, he established the Wolfson Foundation, which had given away £130m to good causes by the time of his death. Wolfson established no fewer than two Oxbridge colleges that bear his name (both for postgraduates), Wolfson College, Oxford (in 1966) and Wolfson College, Cambridge (in 1977). A practising Orthodox Jew and President of the United Synagogue, Wolfson also built 50 synagogues in Israel, including the Great Synagogue on King George Street in Jerusalem. His son Sir Leonard Wolfson, Baron Wolfson (1927–90), continued this record, with the Wolfson Foundation giving away a further £500m by the time of his death. He served as president of the Jewish Welfare Board from 1972 till 1982. The generosity of this family has continued to the present with the current heads of the family, Simon Wolfson, Baron Wolfson of Aspley Guise (b.1967) and Dame Janet Wolfson de Botton (b.1952). Sir Charles Clore (1904–79), who made his wealth in footwear and property, established the Clore Foundation and built the Clore Gallery at Tate Britain. His charitable work was continued by his brother David Clore (1906–85) and by his daughter Dame Vivien Duffield (b.1946), who has headed the Clore Duffield Foundation (as it is now known), which has given away over £200m to charities. The property developer Sir John Ritblat (b.1935) donated the John Ritblat Gallery to the new British Library, which displays its rare books and manuscripts, while Sir Clive Bourne (1942–2007), whose wealth came from an express parcel service, was the founder of the Museum of London Docklands.

Notable philanthropic individuals and families in recent years include such donors as Len Blavatnik (b.1957), the Ukrainian-born entrepreneur who, in 2010, donated £75m to Oxford University to establish a School of Government, the largest gift ever made to Oxford in its history; the Freshwater family – Josias (1897–1976) and Benzion (b. 1948), property tycoons, who have benefited the Charedi community; the controversial businessman Sir Philip Green

(b. 1952); the Pears family, also property tycoons, whose Pears Foundation gave away £17m in 2013–14; the financier Leonard Polonsky (b.1927); Gerald Ronson (b.1939), who gave £40m to charity in the same year; and the advertising entrepreneur Sir Martin Sorrell (b.1945). This brief list obviously does not exhaust the names of notably generous Anglo-Jewish philanthropists of the present, which, of course, is far longer. Many Jews contribute significant amounts to charity anonymously, or to causes that receive little publicity. Studies have shown that up to 90 per cent of British Jews contribute to charity, both for Jewish and general causes, as they have throughout their history in Britain.

Opposite The Sir John Ritblat *Treasures of the British Library Gallery* contains the original manuscript of *Alice's Adventures Under Ground* by Lewis Carroll

are ferrets! Where _can_ I have dropped them, I wonder?" Alice guessed in a moment that it was looking for the nosegay and the pair of white kid gloves, and she began hunting for them, but they were now nowhere to be seen — everything seemed to have changed since her swim in the pool, and her walk along the river-bank with its fringe of rushes and forget-me-nots, and the glass table and the little door had vanished.

Soon the rabbit noticed Alice, as she stood looking curiously about her, and at once said in a quick angry tone, "why, Mary Ann! what _are_ you doing out here? Go home this moment, and look on my dressing-table for my gloves and nosegay, and fetch them here, as quick as you can run, do you hear?" and Alice was so much frightened that she ran off at once, without

"I am proud to be one [British Citizen], just as proud as I am of being a Jew."

(Lionel) Walter Rothschild

Biographies O – S

At age 7, Walter Rothschild told his parents he wanted to open a zoo. He was particularly fascinated by giant tortoises and is seen here riding Rotumah, a Galapagos tortoise that he found living in the grounds of an Australian lunatic asylum.

Florence Oppenheimer

The Jewish Florence
Nightingale *and* Delia Smith
1882–1980

Florence Oppenheimer was born
in north London to Alexander
Oppenheimer and Eliza née Pool.
Her father and her mother's
parents had emigrated from
Holland to the UK. She was
educated at Lady Holles School, a boarding school at Bork-on-Rhine,
for a year and trained to be a nurse at the Royal Sussex Hospital in
Brighton. She served as a nurse in the First World War in the Middle
East and in England and was mentioned in dispatches for her devoted
service in nursing the troops. She has been nicknamed "the Jewish
Florence Nightingale". In 1920 she married Leopold Greenberg, the
editor of the *Jewish Chronicle,* at the West London Synagogue and
embarked upon her second career as a cookery writer. She wrote
a cookery column in the *Jewish Chronicle* from 1920–1962 and
her *Florence Greenberg Cookery Book,* first published in 1934 and
reprinted many times, became a must for every Jewish kitchen. It
contained Jewish, eastern European, British and continental recipes
with small sections on the Jewish dietary laws and traditional Jewish
foods. She also broadcast regularly for the BBC programme *On the
Kitchen Front.* New recipes were added to later editions of her book,
including an interesting banana and spaghetti curry.

Francis Palgrave (né Cohen)

Archivist and executive head of the
Public Record Office
1788–1861

Sir Francis Palgrave was born
Ephraim Cohen in Kentish Town,
the son of Meyer Cohen, a wealthy
stockbroker who later lost his
money. He was educated at home,
and then became a solicitor and
later a barrister. In 1823 he married Elizabeth Turner, at which time he
changed his name to Palgrave (the surname of his wife's mother) and his
religion to Anglicanism. Palgrave had long been interested in medieval
documents and became a noted and widely respected archivist. In
1834 he was appointed Keeper of the Records at the chapter house
in Westminster, publishing deeply researched archival works. In 1838
he was appointed to the key position of Deputy Head and Executive
Director of the Public Record Office (PRO). Palgrave was responsible
for assembling most of England's historical documents and records
in a building in Chancery Lane, which remained the home of the PRO
for 150 years, probably saving thousands of historical documents from
destruction. He was knighted in 1832 and remained in post until his
death. It seems remarkable that a man born as a Jew (and who did not
attend a public school or a university) would at that time be appointed
to a position that, in part, acted to define England's historical identity.
Palgrave had four sons, all of whom became well-known, especially
Francis Turner Palgrave (1824–97), who compiled *The Golden Treasury*
(1861), the best-known anthology of British poetry. None of his sons
were told of their father's Jewish origins until they were adults.

Vladimir Peniakoff
"Popski" of Popski's Private Army
1897–1951

Vladimir Peniakoff was born in Belgium, the son of wealthy émigré Russian-Jewish parents. An excellent student, at the age of 15 he began studying at the University of Brussels, reading engineering, physics and mathematics. Once Germany had invaded Belgium in 1914, Peniakoff was forced to emigrate to England, continuing his studies at St John's College, Cambridge. During his education, Peniakoff was a conscientious objector, but eventually decided to enroll in the French army as a private, rather than training as a British officer. He was wounded in the First World War while working with an artillery unit. Between the two World Wars, Peniakoff worked as an engineer in Egypt, learning Arabic and other languages. In 1940, Peniakoff was commissioned as (possibly the oldest) second lieutenant in the British Army's Libyan Arab Force. By 1942 he was a major, running the Libyan Arab Force Commandos, constantly disrupting Rommel's operations. Eventually dubbed "Popski's Private Army" because of the nickname Peniakoff had been given by the LRDG New Zealanders, Peniakoff's unit would grow and continue to score victories against the Axis forces. Peniakoff was awarded the Military Cross in 1942 and the Distinguished Service Order in 1945.

Maurice Peston
Economist
1931 – 2016

Maurice Harry Peston was born in Stepney, east London. He was the grandson of Jews who had emigrated from Poland and Austria. He was brought up in Hackney but evacuated to Bradford during the war. He was educated at Belle Vue Boys School, Bradford, Hackney Downs School, the London School of Economics (LSE) and Princeton University. He lectured in economics at the LSE and founded the School of Economics and Finance at Queen Mary College, University of London, where he became a professor. Peston was one of the most distinguished economists of his generation. His interest in social justice took him into Labour politics and he served as an economic adviser to many government departments. He was also an ardent supporter of comprehensive education. He became a life peer in 1987 and chaired the House of Lords Committee on Monetary Policy. He also established and chaired the Lords Economic Affairs Committee. Born to Jewish parents, he saw himself as a cultural Jew and an atheist. He became a leading supporter of the National Secular Society and a patron of the British Humanist Association. He married Helen Conroy and was the father of Robert Peston, ITV's political editor. Peston was also a co-founder of the anti-smoking group, ASH.

Marion Phillips
Politician and feminist
1881 – 1932

Born in Melbourne, Australia, the daughter of Philip David Phillips, a solicitor, and Rose Asher, Marion Phillips was educated at Melbourne University. She emigrated to England in 1904, completing a PhD in Australian history – later published as *A Colonial Autocracy* (1909) – and became a lecturer at the London School of Economics and a researcher on the Poor Laws for Beatrice and Sidney Webb. In 1912 she became Secretary of the Women's Labour League and editor of its journal *Labour Women*. Phillips was a significant figure in the British Labour Party, and was appointed its Chief Woman Officer in 1918. She became a Labour councillor in Kensington, and served as Labour MP for Sunderland from 1929–31, the first Australian woman elected to any parliament. She was also the first Jewish woman Labour MP in Britain. She was born to a prominent Jewish family in Melbourne, but described herself as an atheist

Phil Piratin
Communist MP who
resisted the BUF
1907–1995

Phil Piratin was born in
Stepney, London. He attended
Davenant Foundation School.
Throughout the 1930s Piratin
supported a number of local
causes, particularly those
which protected the Jewish districts. He rallied against antisemitism,
organising 100,000 anti-fascists in Cable Street to prevent the
British Union of Fascists (BUF) from marching in 1936. Piratin
also represented tenants trying to get reduced rents and repairs
undertaken in badly maintained accommodation. Piratin was elected
to the Stepney Borough Council in 1937 and was Chairman of the
local Communist Party. His political views prevented him from serving
in the war, but in 1945 he was elected as the Communist MP for the
Mile End constituency. Piratin formed left-wing alliances in the House
of Commons and, with the support of some Labour MPs, managed to
table a Private Members' Bill on safety in employment. But Piratin's
opposition to the Cold War and NATO lost him support, and the
boundary changes ensured that he was not returned to parliament
in 1950. He continued his activism, managing the circulation of the
Daily Worker until 1957 and then starting his own business. He was a
member of the Communist Party GB until its disbandment in 1991.

Leo Pliatzky
Civil servant
1919–1999

Leo Pliatzky was born in Salford, Lancashire, the son of Nathan Plaitzky, a shopkeeper and clothier, and Rose née Portnoy. Both were immigrants from Russia. Pliatzky was educated at Manchester Grammar School, at the City of London School and at Oxford University. During the Second World War he served as a British officer in North Africa and Italy. Pliatzky made a career in the civil service, joining the Ministry of Food from 1947 until 1950, and then the Treasury, rising to Undersecretary (1967–71), Deputy Secretary (1971–76) and Second Secretary (1976–77), and served as Joint Permanent Secretary to the Department of Trade and Industry in 1976–77. He was knighted in 1977. Pliatzky was known for his frank and sometimes abrasive style, especially when arguing for cuts to budgets, particularly during the Labour government of 1974–79. Mrs Thatcher gave him the task of culling "quangos", which he performed successfully. In retirement he was an academic and had business interests.

8∘POALE ZION∘8

Beatrice Plummer
Labour politician
1903–1972

Beatrice Plummer was born to Mayer and Zelda Lapsker of Kiev. She was educated at St George's-in-the-East School, London. In 1923 she married Leslie Plummer, British newspaper executive and politician, who was later knighted. She served as a justice of the peace for Essex from 1947 and was a member of the Police Committee of Essex. In 1965 she was the second Jewish woman to be created a life peer in recognition of her public service. She became Baroness Plummer of Toppesfield, Essex and served as a Labour peer. She was also a member of the board of the Independent Television Authority. Plummer took an active interest in Israel through the Labour Friends of Israel and the Labour Zionist organisations, Poale Zion and Pioneer Women. She was also very interested in agriculture and ran her own arable farm at Berwick Hall, Halstead, Essex. She was a member of the British Agricultural Export Council.

Harry Mayer Primrose
Politician and landowner
1882–1974

Harry Mayer Primrose was the
son of the non-Jewish Archibald
Primrose, 5th Earl of Rosebery
(1847–1929), Liberal Prime
Minister in 1894–5, and Hannah
Rothschild (1851–90, q.v.). Both
of his parents were enormously
wealthy, with his father being a leading Scottish landowner. He
was educated at Eton and Sandhurst and commissioned into the
Grenadier Guards. During the First World War he served as aide-
de-camp and Military Secretary to General Allenby in Palestine, and
had been a Liberal MP from 1906–10. Rosebery sat in the House of
Lords after his father's death in 1929. From May–July 1945 he served
in Winston Churchill's caretaker Cabinet as Secretary of State for
Scotland, although he never held any other government office. He
was also a notable racehorse owner, twice winning the Epsom Derby.
One of the richest men in Britain, he inherited Mentmore Towers,
the great Rothschild mansion in Buckinghamshire, but his heirs were
forced to sell it after his death to pay for death duties.

Sidney George Reilly

"Ace of Spies" and secret agent

c.1874–1925

Sidney Reilly is thought to have been born Salomon Rosenbaum in the Kherson *gubernia* (province) of Russian Ukraine, although this is far from certain, and at least three other plausible accounts of his birth and parentage are known. His father may have been a stockbroker and shipping agent. Targeted by the Tsarist police for his radical activities, the young Rosenbaum went to Brazil, but by 1895 was living in London, now known as Sidney Reilly, selling patent medicines and also working for the British Secret Service. At this point his life becomes even murkier, although it is believed that, while working for the Secret Service, he lived in the Far East, in Russia and in New York. In the First World War he served in the RAF and then became an important anti-Bolshevik agent, attempting to overthrow Lenin. In 1925 he was apparently lured from England to Russia through a "sting" operation by the Bolsheviks and murdered, although, again, this is far from clear. According to reports, during the First World War Reilly came close to assassinating the Kaiser, von Hindenburg, and Erich Ludendorff at a meeting, and came equally close to overthrowing the Bolshevik government in 1918. In the Russo-Japanese War of 1905 he acted as a spy for both sides. He has also been credited with forging the "Voynich Manuscript", the mysterious, allegedly medieval, document that supposedly contains advanced information not generally discovered until much later. Reilly was married four times, but never divorced.

David Ricardo
Economist and politician
1772–1823

Regarded as one of the most important pioneers of modern economics, David Ricardo was born in London, the son of a wealthy Sephardi stockbroker. He was disinherited by his family when he married Priscilla Wilkinson, a Quaker, and subsequently became a Unitarian. Ricardo made an immense fortune as a stockbroker and loan contractor, and served as an MP from 1819 until his premature death four years later. In parliament, he was very significant in influencing government policy in the direction of free trade. Ricardo was known for formulating the concepts in economics of rent, profits and wages, the notion of "diminishing returns" and the "labour theory of value", which heavily influenced Karl Marx. Together with his friend (Revd) Thomas Malthus, Ricardo is credited with giving economics the nickname of "the dismal science."

Cyril Rofe
War hero
1916–1977

Cyril Rofe was born in Cairo, Egypt. Both his parents were Jewish. Educated at Clifton and Chillon College, Rofe trained at the Swiss Hotel School in Lausanne for a career in the hotel business. Employment took him to the May Fair Hotel, London and the Bristol Hotel, Vienna. Rofe fled Austria ten days after the Nazis invaded. He volunteered for aircrew training, but enlisted in the Scots Guard while his application was processed, and joined a special ski battalion destined for Norway. It was disbanded, and Rofe retrained as a bombardier and navigator. In 1941, while on a flight, Rofe's Wellington plane was shot down, crash-landing into the Maas Estuary. The crew were captured. Rofe was sent to the work camp Stalag Luft VIIIB in Lamsdorf. After a failed escape attempt to Switzerland, Rofe made a new attempt in 1944, making it to Russia and joining up with Cossack soldiers. He was later awarded the Military Medal for his escapades and joined the RAF Transport Command as a navigator, flying in the Middle East. Rofe wrote *Against The Wind* (1956) and owned the Escaper restaurant in South Kensington.

Rose Rosenberg
Political secretary
1892–1966

Rose Rosenberg was born in Spitalfields, London in 1892, the daughter of Isaac Rosenberg, a Russian-born tailor, and Rachel née Rosenthal. Trained as a shorthand typist, she became an active suffragette and joined the Fabian Society and, in 1918, the Labour Party. From 1924 until 1937 she served as Private Secretary to Ramsay MacDonald, the first Labour Prime Minister (in 1924 and 1929–31), and then Prime Minister (1931–35) of the national government. She was the second woman to serve a prime minister in this capacity, the first being Frances Stevenson, Lloyd George's private secretary. In Rosenberg's position, she was responsible for managing MacDonald's appointments, reading confidential papers, screening visitors, meeting (or avoiding) reporters and MPs and many other tasks. In 1928, she was the first woman admitted to the Strangers' Dining Room at the House of Commons, and was awarded an OBE in 1930. She later served as an executive of the London branch of MGM Films. Although she knew very many political and personal secrets, she declined to reveal them or write about her career, even many years later. From 1939 until they were divorced in 1954 she was married to Lazlo Hoenig, a refugee from Hungary.

Benny Rothman

Countryside access campaigner
and communist activist
1911 – 2002

Bernard "Benny" Rothman was
born in Manchester, the third of
five children. His parents were
Isaac Rothman, a smallware
merchant, and Freda nee
Solomon. Both were Romanian
emigres. Rothman was educated at Manchester's Central High School
for boys but left at the age of 14 to begin work. With his wages he
bought a bicycle and explored north wales. There the landscape was
a revelation to the city boy, who recalled, "that great open view, with
sea all around". His growing conviction that the countryside was for
all led him to the radical Clarion café in Manchester and membership
of the Young Communist League. In 1932, while staying at the
Communist Party-run British Worker's Sports Federation camp in the
Peak District, Rothman was turfed off the hillside by gamekeepers.
Two weeks later he was back with 400 ramblers in a movement
which became known as the "Kinder Scout Trespass". Rothman, as
ringleader, was imprisoned for four months. In the 1980s Rothman's
countryside access campaign was legitimised by the Rambler's
Association, which had previously distanced itself from the movement.
Rothman appeared on the association's platform numerous times and
his familiar figure – he was stocky and barely five feet tall – inspired a
great deal of affection among countryside lovers.

Ferdinand Anselm de Rothschild

Politician and merchant banker
1839–1898

Baron (of Austria) Ferdinand de Rothschild was born in Paris, the son of Baron Anselm de Rothschild (1803–74), head of the Vienna branch of the famous family. His mother was Charlotte Rothschild (1807–59), the daughter of Nathan Mayer Rothschild, founder of the family's bank in London. Ferdinand de Rothschild lived in England all his life. In 1865 he married a cousin, Evelina de Rothschild (1839–66), daughter of Lionel de Rothschild. Following Evelina's death in childbirth, Rothschild built the Evelina Hospital for Sick Children in London in her memory. He served as a Liberal, later Liberal Unionist, MP for Aylesbury from 1885 until his death. He built the great mansion at Waddesdon Manor, near Aylesbury, Buckinghamshire, in the style of a French chateau, stocking it with rare furniture and works of art. It became an important meeting place for leading politicians, and was visited by Queen Victoria. After his death, he left part of his collection as the "Waddesdon Bequest" to the British Museum, of which he was a trustee. Ferdinand de Rothschild was closely involved in Jewish affairs, and was Treasurer of the Jewish Board of Guardians in 1868 and 1875, and Warden of the Central Synagogue in 1870. Sir Nathan Mayer Rothschild, 1st Baron Rothschild (1840–1915), was his cousin.

Hannah Rothschild
Philanthropist
1851–1890

Hannah Rothschild was the only child of Baron Mayer Amschel de Rothschild (1818–74), a younger son of Nathan Mayer Rothschild (1777–1836), the founder of the British branch of the great merchant bank. Upon her father's death, she inherited much of her father's estate of £2.1m – an astronomical fortune at the time – as well as the princely Rothschild mansion, Mentmore Towers, in Buckinghamshire, and was probably the richest heiress in England. In 1878, at Christ Church, Mayfair, she married the non-Jewish Archibald Primrose, 5th Earl of Rosebery (1847–1929), one of the most prominent younger politicians in the country. The marriage was opposed by both families and was attacked editorially in the *Jewish Chronicle*. Rothschild was given away by Prime Minister Benjamin Disraeli, and the ceremony was attended by the Prince of Wales, but not by any male member of the Rothschild family. She is regarded by historians as an astute political figure on behalf of her husband, and as the main architect of the "Midlothian Campaign" to re-elect William E. Gladstone as Prime Minister. She was also helpful in her husband's political ascendancy – he became Foreign Minister and then Prime Minister, in 1894. Hannah Rothschild was a great patron of charities, including the Club for Jewish Working Girls, but died at only 39 of typhoid and Bright's disease. Rosebery's failure as a politician after the mid-1890s has been traced to his wife's early death. Rothschild eldest son was Harry Mayer Primrose, 6th Earl of Rosebery.

Lionel de Rothschild

First practising Jew to sit as
a member of parliament
1808–1879

Lionel Nathan de Rothschild
was born in the City of London
to Nathan Mayer Rothschild,
a banker, and Hannah Barent
Cohen. The family enjoyed
legendary wealth and Lionel was
a baron of Austria. He was educated at Abraham Garcia's school in
Peckham and at the University of Göttingen. Rothschild joined the
family bank in 1828, and became a partner of the firm in 1836. When
his father died unexpectedly in 1855, he became head of the London
branch of the business. Rothschild was chiefly responsible for raising
large sums for the British government, especially during the Crimean
War. His most famous undertaking was in 1875, when he arranged
a secret loan to the British government to acquire a 44 per cent
interest in the Suez Canal. Rothschild put forward his name as Liberal
MP for the City of London in 1847 but as a Jew, could not take the
Christian oath required to take up his seat in the House of Commons.
It was not until 1858, when the House of Lords agreed to allow each
house to decide its own oath, that Rothschild took his seat as the
first Jewish member of parliament. Apart from a gap of two months
in 1868–69, Rothschild remained an MP until he lost his seat in
1874, achieving his aim of advancing the Jewish cause by entry
into parliament.

Louisa de Rothschild
Philanthropist
1821 – 1910

Louisa de Rothschild was
the fourth child of Abraham
Montefiore and his second
wife, Henrietta Rothschild. Her
father died before she was a
year old and the family spent
long periods in Europe. The
Montefiores eventually settled in London and had a country home
at Worth Park, where Louisa's interest in the welfare of the working
classes began. She helped to start the village school together with
her sister and the local clergyman's widow. In 1840, she married
Anthony Nathan de Rothschild, 1st Baronet from 1847, and they
had two children. Lady de Rothschild supported many philanthropic
causes. Her husband was President of the Jews' Free School and
she was active in the management and knew many of the children
by name. She was a strict observer of the Sabbath but tolerant of
liberal Judaism, and tried to encourage a sympathetic view of Judaism
in non-Jewish friends by sending them literature on Jewish topics.
For many years she maintained a convalescent home in Watford and
sponsored Sabbath classes for girls in what became the West Central
Girls' Club. Her philanthropic and literary interests led to a wide
circle of friends, including Matthew Arnold and Benjamin Disraeli.

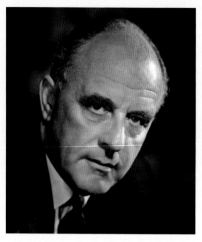

Victor Nathaniel Mayer Rothschild
Government adviser
1910–1990

Victor Nathaniel Mayer Rothschild, 3rd Baron Rothschild, was the son of Charles Rothschild (1877– 1923), a banker and naturalist, who, suffering from encephalitis, committed suicide. His mother was Rozsika von Werthenstein. Victor was educated at Harrow and Cambridge, where he was a member of the Cambridge Apostles, the famous secret society that at that time was dominated by Marxists. Among his friends at Cambridge were the members of the Cambridge Spy Ring. In London, he shared a flat with Guy Burgess and Anthony Blunt, later revealed to be spies for the Soviet Union. As a result, Rothschild was widely suspected in later years of having been the unrevealed "Fifth Man" of the Cambridge Spy Ring, which he strenuously denied. In 1937 he succeeded his uncle as 3rd Baron Rothschild, taking his seat in the Lords – remarkably for a Rothschild – as a Labour peer. During the Second World War he worked for MI5, and later taught zoology at Cambridge, as well as serving on the board of the family bank. He became widely known as the head, from 1971 to 1974, of the Central Policy Review Staff (often known as the "Think Tank"), which undertook research for the Heath and later governments. It provided expert, independent opinions on public issues to the government of the day, but was abolished by Margaret Thatcher in 1983. In later years Rothschild was associated with the Conservative rather than the Labour Party, and was an adviser to several Tory ministers.

(Lionel) Walter Rothschild

Communal leader, merchant
banker and zoologist
1868–1937

Walter Rothschild was the
eldest son of Sir Nathan Mayer
Rothschild, 2nd Baronet, (1840–
1915). He was the grandson of
Nathaniel Mayer Rothschild, the
founder of the renowned merchant
bank, who served as a Liberal MP from 1865–85, and was created 1st
Baron Rothschild, the first professing Jew to be given a peerage. Walter
Rothschild inherited his father's peerage, as 2nd Baron Rothschild, in
1915. He was also a baron of Austria. He was educated at home and
at the universities of Bonn and Cambridge. He worked in the family
merchant bank in London from 1889–1908, and was internationally
known as a zoologist, building up a gigantic collection of natural
history items at his country estate at Tring Park, Hertfordshire. In
1932, he sold much of his collection to the American Museum of
Natural History in New York, to pay – it is said – blackmail money to
a former mistress. The rest of his collection now comprises the Walter
Rothschild Zoological Museum at Tring. There are famous photographs
depicting him sitting on a giant tortoise and driving a carriage drawn
by four zebras. Walter Rothschild served as a Conservative MP from
1899 to 1910. He was an active Zionist and regarded, from about
1915, as the de facto head of the Anglo-Jewish community. The Balfour
Declaration was actually addressed to him, and sent by courier to
his London mansion at 148 Piccadilly. His title passed to his nephew,
Victor Rothschild.

Dick Rubinstein
SOE operative
1921–2005

Richard Arthur Rubinstein was born in London. His father was a milliner, the son of a Latvian Jew. Rubinstein was educated at Hampstead's University College School and Imperial College London, where he read aeronautical engineering. A member of the Territorial Army already, Rubinstein joined the Royal Engineers at the outbreak of the Second World War. In 1941 he became a searchlight officer for the Royal Artillery in Norfolk, overseeing six searchlight sites and 80 men. In 1943 he converted to the Church of England so he could marry Gay Garnsley, but he remained proud of his Jewish roots. Shortly after the wedding, Rubinstein joined the Special Operations Executive, in the Jedburgh team. Known as "The Jeds", they were not so much spies as a liaison force providing munitions, supplies and finance to resistance fighters. In 1944, Rubinstein led a parachute team into Brittany, carrying five million francs, and spent a month hiding in a farmhouse assisting the SAS and FFI to land gliders full of guns. On a later mission, Rubinstein won the Croix de Guerre. In 1944, Rubinstein fought in Burma, organising local militia against the Japanese to great success, winning the Military Cross.

Joseph Samuel Rubinstein

Represented the world of
literature in the world of law
1852–1915

Joseph Samuel Rubinstein was born in Dublin, Ireland. As a young man, he moved with his family to London. After qualifying as a solicitor, he established his own practice along with business partner Daniel Leggatt in 1889. Rubinstein, Nash & Co., as it was later known, became famous for its representation of authors and writers and for dealing with literary libel cases. Rubinstein also published his own works on legal matters. *The Married Women's Property Act* explained the details and consequences of an 1882 parliamentary act that ruled that married women could independently own and control their own property. He also contributed to *Conveyancing Costs*, which ran to multiple editions. Outside of the literary world, Rubinstein founded the Fireproof Fibre Company, which worked to reduce the risk of fire in military buildings. Rubinstein was married to Isabella Alexandra Marks and they had two sons and one daughter. The two sons followed their father into the practice. In 1928, Harold Frederick Rubinstein defended Radclyffe Hall's controversial book *The Well of Loneliness*, throwing the family practice into the glare of publicity.

Michael Rubinstein
Solicitor
1920–2001

Michael Rubinstein was born in Kensington, London, the son of Harold Rubinstein, a solicitor and playwright, and Lina Lowy. He was educated at St Paul's School, and served in the Royal Engineers followed by the Royal Artillery throughout the Second World War. After being demobilised as a captain, he studied law. He subsequently joined the family law firm Rubinstein, Nash & Co. in 1948, where he remained until his retirement in 1994. Rubinstein specialised in representing the leading publishing houses of his era, including Chatto & Windus, Hodder and Stoughton and Penguin Books. His biggest triumph was his successful defence of Penguin Books after charges of obscenity in 1960 following publication of an uncensored edition of D.H. Lawrence's novel *Lady Chatterley's Lover*. Although his hearing had been damaged during the Second World War, Rubinstein's lifelong passion was music and the education of young musicians. He was a director of the company Youth and Music and served the Society for the Promotion of New Music as Trustee, Chairman and then Vice-President. He also published a book, ironically titled *Music to my Ear* (1985). A man with a Judaeo-Christian outlook, he was Honorary Secretary of the Jewish society to aid Arab refugees.

Stanley Rubinstein

Solicitor, author and musician

1890–1975

Stanley Rubinstein was the eldest son of lawyer Joseph Samuel Rubinstein and his wife Isabella Marks. He was born in Kensington, London. After qualifying as a solicitor Rubinstein joined his father's firm, Rubinstein, Nash & Co., which specialised in publishing and copyright law. In later years, Stanley's children and grandchildren also joined the company. Rubinstein was also appointed Chairman of Burke Publishing. In addition to practising law, Rubinstein also wrote his own works, both fiction and non-fiction. One of his most famous books was entitled *The Street Trader's Lot, London 1851*. Published in 1947, the book recorded the true tales of woe and misery of street traders. Rubinstein enjoyed music and became a member of the Worshipful Company of Musicians. He also performed and wrote songs for a small group, the Mixed Pickles. They toured London's youth clubs and put on concerts. In 1969 Rubinstein appeared on the BBC's *Desert Island Discs* where his favourite track was Wagner's *Selig, wie die Sonne* and his luxury item was a family photograph album.

"Power has only one duty –
to secure the social welfare
of the People."

Benjamin Disraeli

Political Pioneers

A painting of Queen Victoria and Prime Minister
Benjamin Disraeli at Osborne House in 1878.
Although Victoria was supposed to be politically
impartial, she preferred the Conservative Disraeli
to his Liberal rival and successor, William Gladstone.

Benjamin Disraeli, illustration by Alfred d'Orsay, 1834

Political pioneers

Daniel Finkelstein
Associate editor of *The Times*
and columnist in *The Jewish Chronicle*

The politics of the Victorian era are usually explained by telling the story of the gradual expansion of the franchise to new social classes and the erosion, as a result, of the power of the landed gentry. But this misses out the other theme, which is the slow change in Britain – starting with the Duke of Wellington's recognition of the need for Catholic emancipation – from being a religious state to being, to all intents and purposes, a secular (if Western) one. In this, the Jews played a crucial role.

Perhaps for this reason, although Jews have been part of the class struggle, for instance in the Communist Party, Jewish political figures have often come from outside this mainstream battle – outside the political establishment – and have taken unorthodox political positions. Perhaps the best (and best-known) example of this is Benjamin Disraeli. Disraeli appreciated that coming from outside the class system was a great weakness in Victorian politics. But he soon began to realise that it can be a great strength. It means you lack identity and can appear alien, but also gives you freedom and room for the imagination.

Disraeli was, his entire life, the victim of antisemitism, even from his Liberal opponents; but at the same time, the perspective of an outsider led Disraeli to the idea of uniting the propertied classes with the workers, using both in alliance to fight the middle-class politics of Robert Peel and of Gladstone. He tied together disparate classes with a very gauzy notion of a romantic Tory democracy. He describes this as best he can in his novels, mixing in his racial ideas. And this introduced Judaism into his political theory. Disraeli argued that Christianity comes from Judaism, together making a superior race. And he suggested that discrimination alone prevented Jews from embracing the "second half" of their Judaism, which is the acceptance of Christ as saviour. It is right to be sceptical of this theory as merely convenient, but also important to note it. Disraeli's ideas about his Judaism and his politics were both creative and subversive. The awkward fact of being a Jew in a Christian nation forces that upon us.

This disconnect was keenly felt by David Salomons, another Jewish political pioneer. In 1851, Salomons stood as a Liberal candidate in a parliamentary by-election in Greenwich and won. Although the Christian parliamentary oath was designed to prevent him from taking his seat, he attempted to take it anyway, and then returned to the Commons in order to vote during the subsequent debate. He was fined £500 for having voted illegally in divisions, but did eventually take his seat in 1859. The struggles of Salomon and Disraeli remind us of just how recently Britain was a resolutely Christian country.

Sir Keith Joseph reached the top of British politics 100 years after Disraeli and lacked any of the latter's pretensions. But I don't think it is too fanciful to argue that being Jewish was part of what made him such an unconventional Conservative. The Thatcherites challenged the class politics and traditions of the Tory party, replacing its leadership and overturning its policies. They introduced ideology in the place of the party's pure tradition and social solidarity. And Keith Joseph was their pioneer.

Joseph was the son of a rich man, 2nd Baronet, educated at Harrow and Magdalen College, Oxford and a captain of the Royal Artillery, mentioned in dispatches. So it is easy to view him as a fairly conventional Tory, arriving on the right of the party from a fairly obvious background. Yet anyone who knew him realised how far he was from being a Conservative cliché. Tortured, intellectual, uncomfortable, he was never a run-of-the-mill party man. Like Disraeli, he helped to challenge the traditional political alignment.

This being in a party but not of it also characterised Edmund Dell, one of my favourites of those given a place in this book. Rising to the top of the Labour Party as a Cabinet minister, Dell challenged his party relentlessly, never quite fitting in, even when he later joined the SDP. In a wonderful book, *A Strange Eventful History*, he is deeply sceptical about the democratic socialism he spent much of his life helping to advance. Is it wrong to detect his Jewish background in this ability to detach himself?

Sir Keith Joseph, of course, was two other things common to Jews in political life. First, he was a lawyer. Again, there is a class explanation available. The law, after all, is a standard profession for those outside the aristocracy who want to use their education to get on. It's a classic field for educated immigrants. But being Jewish has something to do with it, too. It is perhaps a little speculative to argue that there is something about the law that suits the way Jews have been brought up to think. Trying to free up the meaning from texts is our religious tradition, after all. As is trying to interpret rules in a pragmatic way.

It all suits a people of the book, of course. One of the themes of this volume is the role of intellectual endeavour in Jewish success. Leon Brittan (also a barrister) provides an excellent example, building a successful career in politics because his intellectual acuity was so much admired. But less speculative is this: the law is more important to Jews even than democracy. Jews are much safer when judged by a real court than by the court of public opinion.

Sir Keith Joseph, British Government Minister (right),
with philanthropist Fred Worms

Take the life of Hersch Lauterpacht, recently described by Philippe Sands in his magnificent book *East West Street*. Lauterpacht it was who developed the idea of crimes against humanity, the core of the charges against the Nuremberg defendants. Lauterpacht's contention was that states should not be allowed to hide behind sovereignty as a defence against crimes they committed. This now seems conventional, but when he first advanced it it was revolutionary and, indeed, we are still working through its implications. It may be that in a century's time, he will be regarded as one of the most consequential of the Jews on these pages. Sands shows that the idea of crimes against humanity combined the Jewish intellect with the Jewish experience. Lauterpacht was developing a way to prosecute those who murdered his family.

The other thing that Keith Joseph had in common with many other Jews contributing to public life was his business background. Inevitably, given that Jews started outside the establishment, many have been propelled into it by success in commerce, accounting for the prominence of the Wolfson family, the Goldsmids and the Rothschilds.

But where does all of this get us? Is it even useful to note of someone in public life that they were a Jew? Can anything be told from it? Any wisdom gleaned? I think the answer is yes. In style of arguing, in social background, in intellectual endeavour and in reshaping political coalitions as creative outsiders, there is something relevant in noting the Judaism of the subjects in this book. This country has been particularly hospitable to Jews for a number of reasons that become more obvious when you read the biographies contained here.

First, because we, that is the British, have evolved a system where a Christian state can accommodate those who do not accept

Christianity. This has been gradual, beginning in the Victorian era but taking a century to develop.

Second, this is a country in which the law is respected. This protects (reasonably well) the rights of the individual against gusts of public opinion. It has developed into an insistence on civic equality from which Jews gain a great deal.

Third, Britain is an open society that rests on commercial exchange. This allows outsiders to succeed and means the establishment is open to challenge from those born outside the aristocracy of the time.

And finally, this is a stable country without a history of violent overthrow. We have learned to settle arguments with books rather than baseball bats and this is a protection for any minority group.

All of this makes this makes Britain a place where Jews can succeed and live in peace. But will it always be so? Just as the reason for this country being such a hospitable place is obvious from the stories in this book, so are the ways in which that could be undermined. If Britain became a place in which people began to fight their ethnic and religious wars, that would undermine Jewish safety. If we became a place that had less respect for the law and more for temporary public enthusiasms it might make Jewish life less comfortable. If Britons became contemptuous of commerce and banking and trade, more tolerant of violent street protest and more taken by conspiracy theories, the future wouldn't be as good for Jews as the past has been. None of this is impossible. But reading this book should be enough to ensure that Jews aren't just proud of the past, but also optimistic about the future.

Nuremberg Trials, November 1945–October 1946, Courtroom 600 in the Palace of Justice with defendants at left and judges at right

"Whosoever rescues a single soul is credited as though they have saved the whole world."

Talmud, from the Kindertransport Memorial, Liverpool Street station, London

Biographies T – Z

Prominent British citizens including Rabbi Solomon Schonfeld, organised the Kindertransport rescue mission of thousands of Jewish children. Many arrived at Liverpool Street station in the late 1930s.

Leonard Sainer
Successful solicitor
and retail tycoon
1909–1991

Leonard Sainer was born in
London and educated at the
Central Foundation Boys' School
in Islington. He then studied law
at University College London,
becoming a prominent city
solicitor. He was a founding partner of Titmuss Sainer & Webb, set
up in 1938. Sainer became the senior partner of the firm after the
death of Titmuss, and was largely responsible for gaining the firm
the reputation of being one of the best in Britain for retail property
transactions. In 1978 Sainer succeeded Charles Clore, who was
previously a close client, as the chairman of the company Sears
PLC, having helped him to build up the business during the 1950s.
Under Sainer, the company became focused on acquiring new retail
businesses, expanding into continental Europe, and was transformed
into a wide-ranging retailing giant. In 1964 the Leonard Sainer Legal
Education Foundation was set up at UCL in his memory and it ran
until 1989. It awards two scholarships to law students per year. The
Leonard Sainer Centre was also established in accordance with his
wishes, to provide care for Jewish people living with dementia.

Nina Salaman

Hebrew poet, translator, Jewish scholar and feminist

1877–1925

Nina Ruth Davis Salaman was born in Derby to Arthur and Louisa Davis. The family moved to London when she was six weeks old. Salaman's father was a Jewish scholar who had mastered the Hebrew language and he passed this learning on to his two daughters, teaching them at home every day. In her teens, Salaman translated and published medieval Hebrew poetry in the Anglo-Jewish press. She married physician Redcliffe Nathan Salaman in 1901 and after tuberculosis forced him to give up medicine the couple settled in Barley, Hertfordshire, where they lived comfortably in a large country house. Salaman continued with Hebrew poetry and kept a kosher home, while supervising her children's Hebrew education until they went to boarding school. She published *Songs of Exile* by Hebrew Poets in 1901. Salaman was an active member of the Jewish League for Woman Suffrage, campaigning not only to win the vote, but to improve the status of women in the Jewish community and allow women seat-holders to vote in synagogue elections. She encouraged Jewish women to learn Hebrew in order to educate their children. On 5 December 1919, Salaman became the first and only woman to preach in an Orthodox synagogue in Britain. Many of her poems and translations are included in festival prayer books still used today.

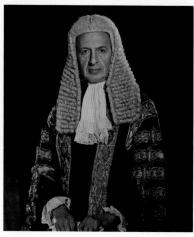

Cyril Barnet Salmon
Judge
1903–1991

Barnett Cyril Salmon was born in London to Montagu Salmon and wife Marian. His father was a tobacconist and co-owned J. Lyons and Co. Ltd., famous for its tea houses. After attending Mill Hill School, Salmon studied law at Pembroke College, Cambridge. He was called to the bar in 1925, the same year that he married his first wife Rencie Vanderfelt. Salmon built up his own successful practice, mainly dealing with civil law cases. Salmon was appointed King's Counsel in 1945. In 1957, he received a knighthood and became a high court judge. He was known for his belief in individual human rights and freedoms. In 1958, Salmon received some notoriety for the tough prison sentences he handed out to the white gang members who had attacked black youths during the Notting Hill race riots. As he passed sentence, he declared "Everyone, irrespective of the colour of their skin, is entitled to walk through our streets in peace, with their heads erect and free from fear." Salmon married his second wife Lady Morris in 1946 and was often seen at public functions with his two daschunds, Rudi and Mimi. Salmon was a member of the Legal Friends of the Hebrew University, Jerusalem.

David Salomons

The first Jewish Lord Mayor
of London

1797 – 1873

David Salomons was born in London. His father, Levy, was a stockbroker. Both Levy and his wife, Matilda de Metz, had come to England from Holland. The family was Ashkenazi and observant. In 1823 David married Jeanette Cohen, a relative of Nathan Mayer Rothschild, and consequently entered the Anglo-Jewish establishment. His new relatives were proponents of Jewish emancipation and Salomons soon joined their cause. Salomons first worked as a banker in the City of London, establishing the London and Westminster Bank. He was considered by many to be an authority on national currency and loans. In 1847 he joined his cousin, Lionel de Rothschild, in standing for parliament. He was elected but when taking the oath upon entering parliament, he omitted the Christian words. For this, Salomons received a number of fines, but he had succeeded in putting the issue on to the political agenda. In 1859, after the passing of de Rothschild's bill that allowed Jews to take a different oath, Salomons was elected to government. After being elected Sheriff of the City of London and High Sheriff of Kent, Salomons became Lord Mayor of London, the first Jew to hold the office.

Joseph Salvador

He petitioned for Jewish
naturalisation in England
1716–1786

Joseph Salvador was born in
London. His father was Francis
Salvador and his mother
Rachel Mendes Da Costa.
Joseph's ancestors had fled
the Portuguese Inquisition and
arrived in London via the Netherlands. Salvador traded in partnership
with his brother Jacob. However, upon Jacob's death, Salvador feared
he would lose his inherited land as he was not a British citizen. As
a result, he lobbied the Duke of Newcastle to put forward an act of
parliament that would allow Jews to be naturalised. The 1753 "Jew
Bill" was passed; however, all the progress was undone at the next
year's general election when the opposition were successful. Salvador
continued to be prosperous and traded in diamonds and bullion.
He was very active within the Jewish community and was appointed
Warden of the Portuguese Synagogue in London from 1746–1765.
He was also instrumental in the founding of the synagogue's infirmary,
Beth Holim. In 1760, upon the establishment of the London
Committee of Deputies of British Jews, Salvador was appointed
secretary and became its president in 1778.

Arthur Samuel

He gave generously
to the city he loved
1872–1942

Arthur Samuel was born in
Norwich to Benjamin Samuel
and his wife Rosetta Haldinstein.
His father and his grandfather's
family were all Ashkenazi Jews.
He was educated in his home
town, attending Norwich School. In 1912 Samuel was appointed
the first Jewish Lord Mayor of Norwich. In the August of that year,
the city experienced devastating floods. Samuel gave generously
to ensure the city's restoration. Samuel stood for parliament in
1918 and was successfully elected MP for Farnham. He held this
seat for almost 20 years, until 1937. During his political career he
held various high-powered offices, including Secretary for Overseas
Trade and Chairman of the Public accounts committee. In 1932 he
was created Baronet Mancroft, and five years later Baron Mancroft.
Arthur Samuel married Phoebe Fletcher in 1912 and his son
Stormont inherited his title.

Herbert Samuel
Cabinet minister and high
commissioner for Palestine
1870–1963

Herbert Samuel was born in
Liverpool to Edwin Samuel, a
banker, and his wife Clara. He was
raised in an Orthodox household
and lived in London. In 1902
Samuel successfully ran as a
Liberal candidate in the Cleveland by-election. Three years later he
was working in the Home Office. Samuel oversaw the Children Act
of 1908. All children were deemed the state's responsibility and
there was an end to child imprisonment. During the First World War,
Samuel formally suggested a British-sponsored centre for Jews in
Palestine. This was the forerunner to the Balfour Declaration. Samuel
was appointed the first British High Commissioner for Palestine in
1920. He received a receipt from the former military commander,
Louis Bols, which read "One Palestine. Complete." Samuel worked
hard to achieve cooperation between Arabs and Jewish immigrants.
This was a difficult task, marred by violence. In 1922 he co-wrote the
white paper that sought to reassure the Arab population while also
reaffirming British commitment to a Jewish state. He left Palestine in
1925 but remained active in politics for the next 40 years.

Samuel Samuel
Politician and businessman
1855–1934

Samuel Samuel was born in London, the son of Marcus Samuel, a shell and curio dealer in the East End. He was the younger brother of Sir Marcus Samuel, 1st Viscount Bearsted (1853–1927), the founder of Shell Transport and Trading, which in 1906 merged with its Dutch rival to form Royal Dutch Shell. The company still exists as one of the largest business firms in the world. Its "shell" symbol, at hundreds of petrol stations, is derived from their father's shell and curio shop in the East End, and is one of the most famous business logos in the world. Bearsted also served as Lord Mayor of London in 1902–3. Samuel Samuel was educated at private schools in London and Paris, and then founded M. Samuel & Co., the merchant bank later known as Hill Samuel. He served as a Conservative MP for Wandsworth and then for Putney from 1918 until his death. Samuel was President of the Jewish Soup Kitchens and other Jewish charities.

Edward Sassoon
MP
1856–1912

Edward Sassoon was born into a well-known and distinguished Jewish family. The Sassoons claimed their lineage back to the Ibn Shoshan family of Toledo, Spain. Edward was born in Bombay to Albert Sassoon and his wife Hannah Moise. His father's family had settled in India after leaving Baghdad. In England, Sassoon served in the Duke of Cambridge's Hussars, rising to the rank of major. He succeeded to father's baronetcy in 1896 and was elected Liberal Unionist MP for Hythe in 1899, serving this constituency until his death. During his time in parliament he was a strong supporter of submarine telegraphy, which enabled cross-ocean communication. He spoke about this issue on several occasions in the House of Commons. Sassoon was elected president of the Sephardi congregation of London in 1902. He also served as Vice-President in the Anglo-Jewish Association and for Jews' College London. He was buried in the Sassoon mausoleum in Brighton. However, the land on which the tomb stood was sold in 1933. It was then converted into a furniture shop, a decorators and most recently, a restaurant.

Philip Albert Gustave David Sassoon

Politician

1888–1939

Sir Philip Sassoon, 3rd Baronet, was born in Paris, the son of Sir Edward Sassoon (1853–1924) and Aline, daughter of Baron Gustave de Rothschild. Known as "the Rothschilds of the East," the Sassoons were Baghdadi Jews who became enormously wealthy as merchants in India and China before settling in London in 1855. Technically a French citizen until the age of 19, Sassoon was educated at Eton and Christ Church, Oxford, and served as Conservative MP for Hythe in Kent from 1912 until his death. This is an extraordinary example of upward social mobility into the establishment of a family who are depicted in a photograph as wearing Baghdadi clothing as late as the 1860s. During the First World War Sassoon was an officer in France, and served – again, most remarkably, given his background – as Private Secretary (1915–18) to Sir Douglas Haig, Britain's Commander-in-chief, and also served as Private Secretary to David Lloyd George when he was Prime Minister (1920–22). Sassoon held the offices of Undersecretary for Air (1924–29 and 1931–37) and First Commissioner of Works from 1937 until his death. He was of major importance in strengthening the RAF just before the Second World War. He was also known for his interest in art, as a collector and museum trustee, and was chairman of the trustees of the National Gallery from 1932 until 1936. Sassoon lived at Port Lympne in Kent and at Trent Park in New Barnet, where he entertained the great and the good from Winston Churchill and Lawrence of Arabia to Charlie Chaplin.

Rabbi Solomon Schonfeld

He helped over 3000 Jews escape from Nazi Germany
1912–1984

Solomon Schonfeld was born in London to Dr Avigdor Schonfeld and his wife Ella Sternberg. He was one of seven children and the family was Orthodox. His father founded the Jewish secondary school movement and Solomon would become its principal in later life. Solomon became Presiding Rabbi of the Union of Hebrew Congregations in London in 1933. That same year, Schonfeld approached the Home Office in order to secure 500 visas for German-Jewish refugees. The refugees were predominately synagogue officials and their families. Through his efforts, he supported the safe passage to England of approximately 1,300 people at that time. After Kristallnacht in 1938, Schonfeld was appointed Executive Director of the Chief Rabbi's Religious Emergency Council. In this capacity, he assisted with the Kindertransport movement, helping another 500 or so children escape Nazi persecution. After the war, Schonfeld travelled, at great risk, to Europe. He wore a mock-military uniform on which he inscribed the Ten Commandments and a Star of David. In Poland and Germany, Schonfeld helped with the rehabilitation of Holocaust survivors. Solomon Schonfeld was posthumously recognised by the British government, who awarded him the title of British Hero of the Holocaust in 2013.

Ben Segal
Intelligence officer and academic
1912-2003

Judah Benzion Segal was born in Newcastle-upon-Tyne, to Moses Hirsch, a rabbi and Hebrew scholar, and Hannah, née Frumkin. Both parents were Latvian immigrants. Segal was educated at Magdalen College, Oxford and St Catharine's College, Cambridge, studying every major Semitic language and gaining a first in oriental languages. He attained a DPhil in 1939 at St John's College, Oxford before starting his Second World War career in public security in Sudan. In 1941 he was posted to Cairo for British Intelligence and a year later began work with the SAS. Segal worked behind enemy lines, spying on Rommel's forces in North Africa, and working with local Arabs. In 1942 Segal was awarded the Military Cross for leading an operation that captured Derna, which proved an important stronghold for General Montgomery's forces. Segal met his wife, Sergeant Leah Seidmann, during the final year of the war in Israel and married in 1946. Leaving the military the same year, Segal returned to academia at University of London. Lecturing in Hebrew and Aramaic, he became a reader in 1955 and Chair in 1961. He was elected a British Academy fellow in 1968. Segal was considered an important scholar of Syriac culture, and was Director of the Leo Baeck College from 1982-85.

Samuel Segal

Doctor and Labour politician
1902–1985

Samuel Segal was born in Mile
End, east London to parents who
had emigrated from Lithuania.
Samuel grew up in Newcastle-
upon-Tyne and was educated
at the Royal Grammar School,
Newcastle, Jesus College, Oxford
and Westminster Hospital. He practised as a doctor at Westminster
and Great Ormond Street Hospitals and served as Senior Medical
Officer and Squadron Leader in the Royal Air Force during the
Second World War. He was a lifelong supporter of the Labour Party
and served as Labour MP for Preston, 1945–1950. In 1964 he was
made a life peer, Baron Segal of Wytham, and from 1973–1982 he
served as Deputy Speaker and Deputy Chairman of Committees in
the House of Lords. He also served as Chairman of the National
Society for Mentally Handicapped Children. Samuel came from
Orthodox rabbinic parentage and he was both a proud Jew and a
supporter of Israel. He became Honorary President of the Oxford
Jewish Congregation and supported many Jewish charities such as
the Anglo-Israel Association and the Anglo-Israel Archaeological
Association. Due to his peerage and his marriage to Molly Rolo, a
native of Alexandria, Samuel was warmly received by President Sadat
in 1977 and subsequently arranged for the transfer of 11 Torah
scrolls from Egypt to Britain.

Arthur Seldon
Paved the way for Thatcherism
1916–2005

Arthur Seldon was born Abraham Margolis in the East End of London. His Jewish parents escaped the pogroms in Kiev at the beginning of the century. They both died in the Spanish flu pandemic of 1918, and Seldon was adopted by a Jewish cobbler. Seldon worked hard to get out of his dire situation and after leaving Raines Foundation School won a scholarship to study at the LSE. He became increasingly interested in free market economics through his reading of Friedrich Hayek and Lionel Robbins, and was a founding member of the Liberal Society. Seldon served in North Africa and Italy during the Second World War and began teaching evening classes at the LSE when he returned. He became the Editorial Director of the Institute of Economic Affairs in 1957, joining Sir Anthony Fisher and Ralph Harris in a hugely influential think tank that helped neoliberalism become the dominant economic ideology in the UK and paved the way for Thatcherism. Seldon's great strength was his ability to make accessible the dense economic ideas proposed by the institute. His book *Capitalism* won the Fisher Arts Literary Prize in 1991.

Beatrice Serota

Labour politician and
social reformer
1919–2002

Beatrice Serota was born
Beatrice Katz in St Pancras,
London. She was the child of
immigrants from Austro-Hungary.
She was educated at Clapton
County Secondary School
and the London School of Economics. She entered local politics
after the Second World War, representing Labour on Hampstead
Borough Council. She then represented Brixton on London County
Council and Lambeth on Greater London Council, where she was
the Chief Labour Whip. She served on numerous committees
relating to education, children, health, housing, crime, maternity and
child welfare. She was appointed a life peer, as Baroness Serota of
Hampstead, for services to children's welfare. She became Minister of
State for Health, 1969–1970; first Local Government Ombudsman,
1974–82 and Deputy Speaker of the House of Lords, 1985–2002.
In 1992 she became a Dame of the British Empire. Beatrice was
strongly committed to her Jewish roots and supported the Labour
Zionist women's group Pioneer Women, which her mother helped to
found. Beatrice co-founded the Hampstead branch of the Council of
Christians and Jews and served as Governor of the Jewish Free School
and Vice-Chairman of the Central Council of Jewish Social Services.

David Sharp

Korean War hero

1928–2016

David Maurice Povolotsky was born in Hackney, London, to parents Samuel and Sadie. The family adopted the surname Powell and relocated to Birmingham, and when Sadie remarried David adopted his stepfather's surname of Sharp. Sharp enlisted in 1945 into the Royal Northumberland Fusiliers. In 1946 he was stationed in the Far East, fighting the Dutch in Indonesia before becoming a jungle warfare instructor in Kota Tinggi, Johor until 1948. In 1950 Sharp was posted to Korea and promoted to battalion intelligence sergeant. He became one of only six British soldiers to be involved with the South Korean Special Forces, gathering intelligence until 1951. Called back to his main unit, Sharp was involved in the 80-hour Imjin River battle and he was eventually captured by the Chinese. Routinely interrogated and tortured, Sharp escaped a number of times, eventually becoming the last POW handed over by the Chinese in 1953. His bravery under such hostile conditions was applauded. Upon his return to England, Sharp was awarded the US Army Commendation with "V" for Valor along with the British Empire Medal. He was also given the Korea Medal of Honor and the United Nations Medal for Korea. Later, Sharp became a troubleshooter for the problems of inner city deprivation. Despite years of fundraising for the Help for Heroes charity, Sharp would have had a pauper's funeral were it not for the kindness of strangers, who crowdfunded his memorial.

Alfred Sherman

Free market proponent who
developed Thatcherism
1919–2006

Alfred Sherman was born in
Hackney, London. His parents
were Russian Jews. Sherman
attended Hackney Downs
School and Chelsea Polytechnic
before joining the republican
cause in the Spanish Civil War. After his eventual capture and
repatriation, Sherman returned to London to study at London
School of Economics, where he was elected President of the student
Communist Party. But his politics underwent a drastic transformation
during his time on the economic staff of the Israeli government in
the 1950s. Sherman became a proponent of free market thinking,
and from 1965 expounded his ideas in the *Daily Telegraph*. He also
criticised the Conservatives' pursuit of traditional Labour policies. In
1971, Sherman became the Conservative councillor for Kensington
and Chelsea, a position he held for seven years. During this time he
began working his friend and Conservative MP, Sir Keith Joseph, to
replace socialism with economic liberalism. The pair joined forces
with Thatcher in 1974 to launch the Centre for Policy Studies, a
vehicle for free market ideas and Conservative think tank. In his role
as director, Sherman had a large influence on the development of
Thatcherism. He was knighted in 1983 but a difference of opinion
with the chair of the CPS Lord Thomas led to his sacking in 1984.

Emanuel "Manny" Shinwell

Trade unionist, Labour minister, a leader of Red Clydeside

1884–1986

Emanuel "Manny" Shinwell was born in Spitalfields, east London, the son of a Polish tailor. His family moved to Glasgow and he worked in the clothing trade, becoming an active trade unionist. A leader of the 40-hour-week campaign, he was jailed for five months for his role in the George Square protest in 1919, and for an inflammatory speech to his seaman's union that led to attacks on black sailors. Elected an MP for the Independent Labour Party in 1922, he lost his seat in 1924 but won a by-election in 1928. He served in the 1929 Labour government but rejected Ramsay MacDonald's national government and lost in the 1931 election, before defeating MacDonald himself in 1935. In 1938 while arguing in support of the Popular Front in Spain, he slapped a Tory MP for an antisemitic insult. In 1945 he became Minister of Fuel and Power, overseeing the nationalisation of the mines, but was blamed for coal shortages during the severe winter of 1947 and demoted. He was also accused of passing secrets to Zionist paramilitaries. He was Minister of Defence from 1950–51, and remained active in the Commons and later the Lords, until his death aged 101.

John Silkin

An outspoken early
critic of the EU
1923–1987

John Silkin was born in London
to solicitor Lewis Silkin (later
Baron Silkin) and his wife Rosa
Neft. His father served as
Minister for Town and Country
Planning in Clement Atlee's
post-war Labour government, a post John would also hold later in
life. He was educated at Dulwich College and then at Trinity Hall,
Cambridge. After serving in the Far East during the war, John trained
as a solicitor. He qualified in 1950. In 1963, on his fourth attempt,
John Silkin entered parliament as Labour MP for Deptford. During his
parliamentary career, he distinguished himself as an outspoken critic
of the European Community. In his post at the Ministry of Agriculture,
he regularly clashed with Brussels officials over British fishing rights
and other agricultural issues. This stance proved popular with a large
part of the British public. In 1980, following Callaghan's resignation,
Silkin stood for the Labour leadership. He may have overestimated
his popularity, however, as he was unsuccessful in the first round of
voting. Silkin married actress Rosamund John in 1950, and the couple
had one son, Rory, in 1954.

Lewis Silkin

Minister of Town and Country
Planning under Clement Attlee
1889–1972

Lewis Silkin was born in Poplar,
east London to Lithuanian-
Jewish parents. His father was
a Hebrew teacher and grocer.
Silkin was educated at the
Central Foundation School, then
attended East London College. Despite winning a mathematical
exhibition to Worcester College, Oxford, he went to work in the
East India docks instead. He then became a clerk to a solicitor and
qualified as a solicitor himself before setting up his own law practice,
now known as Lewis Silkin LLP. In 1925, Silkin was elected to the
London County Council for South-East Southwark and became
leader of the opposition Labour group on the LCC in 1930. He
became Chairman of the Housing and Public Health Committee
in 1934 and two years later, was elected to parliament as Labour
member for the Peckham division of Camberwell in a by-election. He
was appointed Minister of Town and Country Planning by Clement
Attlee in 1945, a position he held until his retirement in 1950. In this
role, Silkin was responsible for implementing the Town and Country
Planning Act (1947), which enabled local authorities to conserve
buildings of historic interest, and also brought in the National
Parks and Access to the Countryside Act (1949), which created 10
national parks. He was created Baron Silkin in 1950.

Samuel Silkin

A supporter of the
European Community
1918–1988

Samuel Charles Silkin was born
in Neath, Glamorgan to solicitor
Lewis Silkin (later Baron Silkin)
and his wife Rosa Neft. His
father's family had settled in
Britain after emigrating from
Lithuania in the 19th century. After attending Dulwich College and
Trinity Hall, Cambridge, Silkin was called to the bar by the Middle
Temple in 1941. That same year he married Elaine Violet née Stamp.
Like his father before him, and later his brother John, Silkin stood
for parliament as a Labour MP. He was elected in 1964 for the
constituency of Camberwell, Southwark. Unlike his brother John
Silkin, Samuel was a great supporter of the European Community.
From 1968 to 1970 he led the British delegation to the Council
of Europe. He was appointed Attorney General in 1974 by Harold
Wilson. However, Silkin refused the knighthood that accompanied the
appointment. Thus, he dismissed a 400-year-old tradition.
Silkin was a great cricketer, representing both Glamorgan and
Cambridge in first-class games. He was proud of his Jewish heritage,
and was associated with the Friends of the Hebrew University,
Jerusalem, the Association of Jewish Ex-Servicemen and other Jewish
community organisations.

John Simon

He defended the rights
of Jewish citizens abroad
1818–1897

John Simon was born in Montego Bay, Jamaica. His father Isaac was a merchant. His mother, Rebecca, was descended from the Spanish Orobio family. Balthasar Orobio had been imprisoned during the Spanish Inquisition, and his father Caesar had been burned at the stake as a result of his Jewish faith. After receiving a British education, Simon graduated from the University of London with a law degree in 1841. A year later he was called to the bar, the second Jew to ever be admitted. During his legal practice, he successfully defended Simon Bernard against charges of complicity in an assassination attempt on Napoleon III. In 1864 John Simon was appointed Serjeant-at-Law. Four years later, Simon was elected Liberal MP for Dewsbury, Yorkshire. He was a skilled orator and defended the rights of MPs to speak in parliament without taking the traditional oath. Simon was passionate about Jewish affairs, especially in regards to the welfare of Jews abroad. In 1870, he organised the Mansion House meeting that condemned the treatment of Jews in Romania and Serbia. He was outspoken about the anti-Jewish pogroms in Russia during the late 1880s. In 1886 he received a knighthood. He was buried in Golders Green Cemetery.

Krystyna Skarbek
Super Spy
1908–1952

Maria Janina Krystyna Skarbek (alias Christine Granville) was born in Warsaw. Her father was Count Jerzy Skarbek and her mother was Stephania Goldfeder, daughter of a wealthy Jewish banker. Krystyna was a "tomboy"; she could ride and ski and developed a spirit of adventure. After leaving convent school she took a job at a Fiat garage, but was forced to leave when exhaust fumes began to affect her lungs. Seeking a healthier outdoor life, she moved to Poland's Tatra Mountains. She married Jerzy Gisycki and in 1938 moved with him to colonial Kenya. Upon the outbreak of war the Gisykis made their way to London, determined to do their bit to fight the common enemy. Skarbek volunteered for the intelligence services and her potential was recognised at once. She was sent to Hungary to establish lines of communication with her native Poland. With the help of Olympic skier Jan Maruzarz, she skiied over the mountains and connected disparate intelligence cells on either side of the border. On a trip to Warsaw she attempted – unsuccessfully – to extract her Jewish mother from Poland. Stephania was later arrested and murdered by the Gestapo. Skarbek herself was arrested in 1941, but escaped by feigning tuberculosis. Skarbek was awarded the George Cross for her war work. She later worked on an ocean liner and was murdered by fellow steward Dennis Muldowney while on shore leave in an Earl's Court hotel. Skarbek was buried in an Anglican cemetery. She is said to have been the inspiration for Ian Fleming's femme fatale Vesper Lynd in the novel *Casino Royale* (1953).

Archibald Levin Smith
A well-liked and respected judge
1836–1901

Archibald Levin Smith was born in Salt Hill, Sussex, to Francis Smith and his wife Mary Ann Lee. Although he had Jewish ancestry, he was baptised into the Christian faith as a child. After being home-schooled, Smith studied law at Trinity College, Cambridge. At university, he was a successful oarsman and competed in the annual boat race between 1857 and 1859. On the last of these races, he had to be rescued when the boat sank as he could not swim. In 1860 he was called to the bar and was well liked and respected on the circuit. In 1883, he was appointed a judge of the Queen's Bench Division and received a knighthood. In 1888, alongside Mr Justice Day, Smith served on Sir James Hannen's tribunal, which investigated allegations against Charles Stewart Parnell and other Irish nationalists. In 1892, he was promoted to the court of appeal. Shortly after being made Master of the Rolls, Smith encountered personal tragedy. His wife, Isabel, drowned in the River Spey in August 1901. He never got over the shock and died less than three months later.

Issy Smith
Victoria Cross winner
1890–1940

Issy Smith was born Ishroulch Shmeilowitz in Alexandria, Egypt to French-Jewish parents. At 11 he came to London as a stowaway on a ship and attended the London County Council School, Whitechapel. In 1904, aged 14, he joined the Manchester Regiment and later won the army middleweight boxing championship. In 1912 he left the army and emigrated to Australia but was recalled for army service in August 1914. In April 1915 during the second battle of Ypres in Belgium, Smith showed outstanding bravery in rescuing a wounded man under enemy fire and carrying him 250 yards to safety. Later the same day he rescued more wounded men under heavy fire. These actions gained him the Victoria Cross, presented to him by King George V. Later in Mesopotamia he received the Tsarist medal of St George for rescuing Russian soldiers. Smith visited different Jewish communities in Britain after receiving the Victoria Cross to stimulate further recruitment. In 1919 he married Elsie Porteous Collingwood McKechnie at Camberwell Registry Office. Although the ceremony was later solemnized according to Jewish rites, Smith's parents disowned him for marrying outside the faith, and the newlyweds emigrated to Australia. In 1940 he was given a Jewish burial with full military honours. During the course of the First World War Smith had been gassed, and wounded five times.

Henry Solomon
Brighton's first Chief Constable
1794–1844

Henry Solomon started life
as a watchmaker in London.
In 1838, he was appointed
Chief Constable in Brighton, a
remarkable achievement in a
time when Jews often suffered
discrimination. Solomon led
a police force of 31 officers in the Brighton community. He is,
unfortunately, best known for his untimely demise. Solomon was
questioning 23-year-old John Lawrence, a young thief who had
been arrested for stealing a carpet roll. Mid-interview Lawrence
bludgeoned Solomon over the head with a poker. It is believed
he is the only Chief Constable to have been murdered in his own
police station. An appeal was launched to raise money for Solomon's
widow and nine children and attracted a large number of donations,
including £50 from Queen Victoria. Lawrence was publicly hanged
at Horsham after being found guilty of murder at Lewes Assizes.
Solomon has posthumously taken on celebrity status in Brighton.
His grave in the Florence Place Old Jewish Burial Ground is a tourist
attraction and in 2004 a new bus fleet was named after him.

Harold Benjamin Soref
Politician
1916–1993

Harold Benjamin Soref was born
in Hampstead, the son of a
Romanian-born African merchant.
He was educated at St. Paul's
School and at Oxford, and during
the Second World War served
in the Royal Scots and in the
Intelligence Corps. During the 1930s he provided the Jewish Board
of Deputies with information about the British Union of Fascists, and
was forcibly ejected from Sir Oswald Mosley's notorious Olympia
Rally of 1934. From 1947–51 Soref was the editor of the *Jewish
Monthly*. From 1970–74 he served as Conservative MP for Ormskirk.
On the right wing of the party, he was a stalwart of the Monday Club
and had strong business links with Southern Rhodesia. He was also a
staunch supporter of Israel and, during the Yom Kippur War of 1973,
voted against the Heath government's refusal to sell spare tank parts
to Israel. Soref was in the news during the 1970s for escaping from a
left-wing mob at Oxford by scaling a wall, and for narrowly avoiding
being assassinated by the IRA outside his flat in Chelsea, when an
innocent bystander was murdered in his stead.

Linda Joy Stern
British QC, prosecutor and judge
1941–2006

Linda Joy Stern was born in London, the daughter of Lionel Hart and Lily Rachel Gold. She was educated at St Paul's Girls' School. In 1971, she was called to the bar at Gray's Inn. A year later, she became the first woman tenant at the Red Lion Chambers. From 1990–2001 Stern was a recorder of the crown court. She was appointed a QC in 1991. Her best-known case was as prosecutor in the Victoria Climbie murder trial in 2001. In 1993 she was elected a fellow of the Royal Society of Arts.

Sidney Stern

Millionaire banker whose
generosity benefited both
young and old
1845–1912

Sidney Stern was born in London
to David Stern and wife Sophie,
who was the niece of Sir Isaac
Lyon Goldsmid. Sydney's father
was a viscount of Portugal who
had lived in Frankfurt before coming to England. Sidney was educated
at Magdalene College, Cambridge and was also admitted to the Inner
Temple in 1874. He worked for some time in his father's merchant
banking firm, Stern Brothers. However, he later decided to pursue a
political career. He was elected Liberal MP for Stowmarket in 1891.
He served this constituency until he was named Baron Wandsworth
in 1895. It was later proven that his baronetcy was largely due to
the significant financial contribution he had made to the Liberal
Party. Sidney Stern had no heir when he died in 1912. He therefore
chose to leave a vast sum of money (over £1m) for the establishment
of a new school in Stowmarket. The school, now known as Lord
Wandsworth College, was to be for the children of agricultural
workers, or for those who had lost parents. Observant in his faith,
Stern also gave generously to the Jewish community. He made a
financial contribution to the establishment of the Jewish Home for
the Aged in Wandsworth, which was opened in 1910. His cousin
Herbert Stern was created 1st Baron Michelham.

Peter Stevens

RAF recipient of the
Military Cross
1919–1979

Peter Stevens was born Georg
Franz Hein in Hanover, Germany
to a Jewish family. He attended
boarding school in Germany and,
from 1934, in England. Wanted
by the police for gambling debts,
Stevens adopted a false identity. He joined the RAF and flew 22
combat operations during 1941 before being shot down and taken
as a prisoner of war. For over three years he attempted many escapes,
one from a moving train. In camp Oflag V1-B he twice disguised
himself as a German officer and led disguised orderlies and guards
out of the camp, only to be turned back at the gate. This attempt
was described as "The War's Coolest Escape Bid" by London's *Evening
Chronicle*. Later in camp Oflag XX1-B he escaped through a tunnel
but was eventually captured. At Stalag Luft 3 he became the head
of contacts, scrounging materials for planned escapes. Liberated
by the Russians in 1945, he returned to England and was awarded
the Military Cross. From 1947 he worked for MI6 for five years
in Germany and then emigrated to Canada. He married a French
Canadian Catholic and never told his family he was Jewish. The
character of "The Scrounger" in the film *The Great Escape* was
partly modelled on Stevens.

Julius Stone

First academic lawyer
to become a QC
1907–1985

Julius Stone was born in Leeds,
England. His parents were refugees
from Lithuania. He was educated
at Leeds Central High School and
then studied jurisprudence at
Exeter College, Oxford, where he
was involved in the Inter-University Jewish Federation of Great Britain
and Ireland. He went on to study for an MA in law at Leeds University,
followed by a doctorate of juridical science at Harvard University. Stone
returned to England in 1936 and became a lecturer at Leeds University.
In 1938, he was appointed Dean of Law at Auckland University
College, and moved to New Zealand, becoming President of the New
Zealand League of Nations Union two years later. In 1942, Stone was
appointed to the chair of jurisprudence and international law at the
University of Sydney. Despite opposition among staff to Stone's radical
teaching stance and Jewish identity, he remained there until 1972. In
1946, he penned his first book, *The Province and Function of Law*, which
established him as a leading scholar of law and won him the Swiney
Prize for jurisprudence. In 1972, he moved to the University of New
South Wales as a visiting professor, where he remained until his death.
He was awarded an OBE in 1973, and was appointed a QC in 1982 –
a unique accomplishment for an academic lawyer.

Opposite Peter Stevens was the inspiration for James Garner's character 'The Scrounger'
shown here with Donald Pleasance in *The Great Escape*, 1963

George Strauss
Politician who ended
theatre censorship
1901–1993

George Strauss was the son of
Arthur Isidor Strauss (1847–
1920) and Minna Cohen. His
father was a wealthy copper
and tin merchant in the City
of London, who had served as
a Liberal Unionist MP (1895–1900), then as a Conservative MP
(1910–18), and, curiously, then joined the left-wing Independent
Labour Party. George Strauss was educated at Rugby, where he
experienced a good deal of antisemitism. After leaving school he
also became a metal merchant. He served on the London County
Council and was also elected as a Labour MP twice in his career. He
was temporarily expelled from the party in 1939 for supporting a
"popular front" with the Communists, but held office in the Attlee
Labour government as Parliamentary Secretary to the Ministry of
Transport and then as Minister of Supply, where he piloted through
the nationalisation of the steel industry. He did not hold office again;
but in 1968 he secured the end of theatre censorship. From 1974
through 1979 he was the "Father of the House," the longest-serving
MP. He was given a life peerage in 1979 as Baron Strauss. He had no
direct involvement with the Jewish community.

Peter Taylor

Undertook inquiry into the
Hillsborough disaster
1930–1997

Peter Taylor was born in
Newcastle-upon-Tyne, into a
Jewish family originally from
Lithuania who had anglicised
their surname from Teiger
or Teicher. His mother came
from a notable rabbinical family. Taylor was educated at the Royal
Grammar School in Newcastle and went on to study law at Pembroke
College, Cambridge. He was called to the bar in 1954 and took silk
in 1967. His two most notorious cases were the prosecutions of the
architect John Poulson in 1974 and of Liberal Party leader Jeremy
Thorpe in 1979. In 1972, he became Recorder of the Crown Court.
He was made a full high court judge in the queen's bench division in
1981, and received a knighthood. In 1989, he was commissioned to
undertake an inquiry into the Hillsborough disaster and subsequently
produced the Taylor Report, which led to the introduction of all-
seater stadiums at top English football clubs. His reputation as a fair
judge led to his appointment as Lord Chief Justice in 1992. He was
the first judge to appear on BBC's *Question Time* and on BBC Radio
4's *Desert Island Discs*. Despite once describing himself as "out on
a long leash from Judaism", he led delegations of Jewish lawyers on
visits to Israel and remained in touch with his roots.

Robert Stanford Tuck
RAF Wing Commander
1916–1987

Roland Robert "Bob" Stanford Tuck was born in Catford, London. He was educated at St Dunstan's College, Reading. In 1935 he joined the RAF, becoming a pilot officer, and in 1940 he was promoted to flight commander flying Spitfires. He was in combat over Dunkirk and in the Battle of Britain and became Squadron Leader flying the Hawker Hurricane. Stanford Tuck was awarded the Distinguished Flying Cross (DFC) by King George VI in June 1940, a bar to his DFC in October 1940, the Distinguished Service Order in January 1941, and a second bar to his DFC in March 1941. He had been successful at shooting down a total of 22 enemy aircraft. 'Tuck's Luck' became a well known phrase in the RAF of the early 1940s; but in 1942 the luck ran out. He was shot down and taken to the prisoner-of-war camp, Stalag Luft 111, but not before his captors, impressed by Tuck's sharp shooting, had taken him to lunch. He made several escape attempts, finally succeeding in February 1945. He fought alongside the Russians before reaching the British embassy in Moscow and returning to England. Stanford Tuck retired from the RAF in 1949 having reached the rank of wing commander. In 1953 he settled with his wife and sons in Kent and successfully farmed mushrooms for 20 years. Stanford Tuck was profiled in the Jewish Chronicle in 1941, and throughout his active service he carried a Jewish Chaplain card, but his own sons were unaware of his Jewish origins.

Chaim Weizmann

Made a nation for the Jews as
the first president of Israel
1874–1952

Chaim Weizmann was born in
Motol, Russia in the Jewish Pale
of Settlement. His father, Ozer,
occasionally led the prayers
at the local synagogue and
brought Chaim up in a traditional
Jewish household. Chaim was blocked from attending university in
Russia so instead studied in Germany and Switzerland, receiving his
doctorate from the University of Fribourg. He became increasingly
involved in Zionist societies and was influential in the Russian-Jewish
Academic Society. He joined Manchester University in 1904 and
became very loyal to Britain, coming to the country's aid in 1915
to provide a cheap way of producing acetone for explosives. This
won Weizmann the favour of the government, giving him leverage to
negotiate the 1917 Balfour Declaration in recognition of the Zionist
claims on Palestine. Weizmann became leader of the World Zionist
Organisation in 1920 and worked tirelessly to create a homeland
and forge a sense of Jewish national identity. Crucial to this aim was
his Hebrew University, which opened in 1925. Weizmann became
President of the new Jewish state of Israel in 1948. He gave up his
British citizenship the following year and became a citizen of Israel.

Jack White
Victoria Cross winner
1896–1949

Jack White was born Jacob Weiss in Leeds to parents from Austria and Russia. He grew up in Edinburgh and Salford. He joined the Royal Lancaster Regiment in 1914 and was attached to the 13th Western Division. He served in Gallipoli and then joined the Tigris Corps. In 1917 he won the Victoria Cross for conspicuous bravery and resource. While pontoons of his unit were crossing a river they came under heavy fire and when Jack's pontoon reached midstream every man except himself was dead or wounded. Unable to control the pontoon, he jumped overboard and towed it to shore using a telephone wire, saving the life of an officer as well as valuable equipment. He was also awarded the Italian Bronze Medal of Military Valour. Jack returned to Manchester and entered the clothing trade. He was a proud Jew and established Jewish branches of the British Legion, actively worked for the Jewish Lads Brigade and served on the Council of Manchester and Salford Jews. His heroics were shown in *Victor* comic in 1987 and this comic strip is printed on the tissue paper used to wrap the orders of the clothing firm Private Jack White VC, run by his great-grandson in the factory he owned.

Nicholas Winton
Rescue worker dubbed
the "British Schindler"
1909–2015

Nicholas Winton was born
in Hampstead, London. His
parents were wealthy Jewish
immigrants from Germany, who
changed their family name
from Wertheim and converted
to Christianity in a bid to integrate with British society. Winton was
baptised. He attended Stowe School before becoming a London
stockbroker. In 1938, Winton's friend Martin Blake invited him to
Prague to meet members of the British Committee for Refugees from
Czechoslovakia. The city had become a refuge for people fleeing the
advancing Germans, but they lived in terrible conditions. Winton was
determined to alleviate the situation and began collecting details
and photographs of the families. He returned to London with his list
of refugees and there worked tirelessly to arrange safe crossings to
England. He was forced to overcome many bureaucratic obstacles,
sometimes forging Home Office papers to ensure children were let in.
Winton and his team saved nearly 700 children before the outbreak
of war. He remained a secret hero until his wife Grete discovered his
scrapbook with the children's details. Many of the people he rescued
were finally able to thank him at the broadcast of BBC's lifestyle
show *That's Life* in 1988. Presenter Esther Rantzen asked the studio
audience to "stand up if you owe your life to Nicholas Winton". Every
single audience member did so, and Winton found himself embraced
by the survivors whose lives he had saved.

John Wiseman
SAS soldier
1916–2005

John Martin Wiseman was born in Kingston-upon-Thames, Surrey, to German-Jewish father Max, a spectacles salesman. Wiseman was educated at St Paul's School and then Cambridge, reading history and modern languages. He joined his father's company in 1937, but at the outbreak of the Second World War he enlisted as a trooper with the North Somerset Yeomanry, fighting in Syria against the Vichy French. Sent to Cairo in 1942, Wiseman enlisted in the SAS and caused disruption for German transport by mining roads and attacking the Tobruk–Mersa Matruh railway. In 1943 Wiseman led a section to raid Cape Murro di Porco, Sicily. The mission was a huge success, and Wiseman was awarded a Military Cross for his leadership. Shortly after, he narrowly escaped death when his unit's truck was shelled, killing his men. Promoted to captain, in 1944 Wiseman took part in Operation Houndsworth, part of the invasion of France, and was awarded the Croix de Guerre with Silver Star.

Milly Witkop

Feminist writer, activist
and anarcho-syndicalist
1877–1955

Milly Witkop was a Jewish
Ukrainian, born in Zlatopol
to Simon Witkop (Shimon
Vitkopski), and his wife Freda
Grill. She moved to London and
saved enough money, working
in an East End sweatshop, for her family to join her in 1895. The
family was observant, but Witkop and two of her sisters became
disillusioned and broke away from both the religious and political
views of their parents. Witkop and her sister Rose became involved
in the anarcho-syndicalist movement, which many Jewish workers
supported. Through the organisation, she met her life partner
Rudolf Rocker (1873–1958), a German political activist, in 1895.
Witkop and Rocker co-edited *Der Arbeyter Fraynd* (The Worker's
Friend), the Yiddish anarchist paper, although Rocker was not Jewish.
In 1898, Witkop accompanied Rocker to the United States, but
they were refused entry because they were unmarried. She told the
authorities, who had accused them of promoting free love, that love
was always free and when it was not, it was prostitution. In 1920,
Witkop was one of the founders of the Berlin Women's Union and
the Syndicalist Women's Union. Witkop and Rocker's son was the
artist Fermin Rocker.

Maurice Wohl
Property developer
and philanthropist
1917–2007

Born in the East End of London
to parents of eastern European
origin, Maurice Wohl became a
property developer at a young
age. He founded his company
United Real Property Trust
in 1948 and built up a considerable property portfolio of office
building in London's West End and the City. His company was floated
on the Stock Exchange in 1961, and, encouraged by his father
who had trained as a rabbi and instilled in him the spirit of giving,
he established the Maurice Wohl Charitable Foundation in 1965.
In 1974 he retired from the business, and with his wife Vivienne
he divided his time between Geneva, Tel Aviv and London, and
devoted himself to collecting art and other cultural pursuits, and to
philanthropic activities. He made donations both in a private capacity
and through three public charitable foundations supporting medical
science, welfare and education. He gave substantial sums to medical
research in the UK, and to medical, educational and religious causes
in Israel. He was President of the Jerusalem Great Synagogue, and
was a generous supporter of Bar-Ilan University. He was awarded
the title of "Trustee of Jerusalem" by Mayor Ehud Olmert, and was
appointed a Commander of the British Empire in 1992.

Vivienne Wohl
Philanthropist
1945–2005

Born Vivienne Horowitz, she was the daughter of friends of future husband Maurice, and worked as an assistant in his office before they were married in Jerusalem in 1966. In contrast to her private and reserved husband, she was gregarious and extrovert. Vivienne and Maurice Wohl spent more than 40 years of their life together supporting charitable causes in the UK and in Israel, and contributing to Jewish communities in central and eastern Europe and around the world. Typical of their joint efforts are the Maurice and Vivienne Wohl Philanthropic Foundation, established in their lifetimes to make grants for the advancement of medical science, social and communal welfare and education; and the Maurice and Vivienne Wohl Charitable Foundation, which supports Jewish people in Israel, the former Soviet Union and wherever they are in need. They also gave support to individuals privately, often seeking people out they had read about in newspapers and tracking them down to offer support. Vivienne died of cancer in 2005, two years before her husband. After their deaths, the Maurice and Vivienne Wohl Campus in Golders Green was funded from the sale of their artworks, providing for the elderly and those in need, including Holocaust survivors. The site features a community centre for the wider public offering a range of social and therapeutic activities, and a state-of-the-art facility providing care for the elderly and those in need. Priority is offered to Holocaust survivors and those who fled Nazi persecution.

Lucien Wolf

Communal leader, journalist
and advocate of Jewish rights
1857–1930

Lucien Wolf was born in London,
the son of Edward Wolf, a pipe
manufacturer, and Céline Redlich.
He was educated at Highbury College
and at institutes in Brussels and Paris,
where he became multilingual. Wolf
was Foreign Editor (1890–1909) of the *Daily Graphic* newspaper, and
Editor (1906–8) of the *Jewish World*. He became an internationally known
campaigner against Tsarist antisemitism, and also wrote the article on
Antisemitism in the 11th (1911) edition of the *Encyclopaedia Britannica*.
Wolf became Secretary of the Co-Joint Foreign Committee of the Anglo-
Jewish Association and of the Board of Deputies, and was widely regarded
as the informal "Foreign Secretary" of Anglo-Jewry. He played a major and
important role at the Paris Peace Conference in 1919 in securing rights for
minorities in the newly created states of eastern Europe, most of which
had large Jewish populations. Although these rights were secured on paper,
it became increasingly difficult to enforce them as the tide of local ultra-
nationalism grew in the 1920s. (Wolf did not live to see the rise of Nazi
Germany.) Wolf also staunchly opposed the Balfour Declaration and the
Zionist movement, although he supported campaigns by Israel Zangwill
and other "territorialists" to secure a Jewish homeland elsewhere than in
Palestine. He wrote very widely on Jewish history and affairs; his *Essays on
Jewish History*, edited by Cecil Roth, appeared posthumously in 1934. Wolf
organised the important Anglo-Jewish Historical Exhibition of 1887 and
was the first president of the Jewish Historical Society of England.

Isaac Wolfson

Philanthropist and
mail-order magnate
1897–1991

Born in the Gorbals, Glasgow,
Isaac Wolfson's father Solomon
was a cabinet maker who had
fled from Poland. With an
aptitude for mathematics, but
unable to afford to train as an
accountant, Wolfson became a successful salesman for his father. In
1931 he went to work for Great Universal Stores and soon acquired
a majority shareholding, becoming Managing Director in 1934. He
built the company up to become a major mail-order business, and
in the process became extremely wealthy. A devout Orthodox Jew,
he is quoted as saying: "No man should have more than £100,000.
The rest should go to charity". In 1955 he established the Wolfson
Foundation, whose priorities were promoting health, medical and
scientific research, education, history, the arts and youth projects.
Among the major projects supported by the foundation were
providing halls of residence and establishing a Wolfson College at
both Oxford and Cambridge, the latter the first at that university
to admit both men and women. The foundation also supported
a number of Israeli universities, and medical research institutes in
Glasgow, London and Newcastle. Wolfson also famously donated
£100,000 in 1961 to buy the Goya portrait of the Duke of
Wellington on behalf of the nation. In 1962 Wolfson received
a baronetcy in the New Year's Honours list, becoming Sir Isaac
Wolfson of Marylebone.

Leonard Gordon Wolfson

Businessman and philanthropist
1927–2010

Leonard Gordon Wolfson was born in London, the son of Sir Isaac Wolfson whose father was a Russian-Jewish immigrant to Glasgow. Leonard was educated at the King's School, Worcester. He joined his father in the highly successful mail-order business Great Universal Stores, of which he became Chairman in 1982. He streamlined the business, sold off the general high street retail side and concentrated on finance, property and mail order. He helped to establish the Wolfson Foundation in 1955 for the advancement of medicine, science, health, education, the arts and humanities, becoming Chairman in 1972. The foundation donated money to the Wolfson Colleges in Oxford and Cambridge and has distributed over one billion pounds to numerous causes. Leonard was knighted in 1977, created a Conservative life peer in 1985 as Lord Wolfson of Marylebone, and he inherited his father's baronetcy in 1991. He was a loyal Jew, if not as observant as his father, and a great supporter of projects in Israel. He was Chairman of the Jewish Welfare Board and a member of the Central Synagogue, London. As a young man, he went to Israel during the War of Independence to show solidarity with the young country at what he perceived to be a crucial moment. He loved classic film, cricket and history.

Edith Zangwill
Novelist and suffragette
1875–1945

Edith Ayrton Zangwill, born
in Japan, was the daughter of
distinguished physicist William
Edward Ayrton and his wife
Matilda Chaplin, a pioneering
doctor. Edith was educated
at Bedford College, London
University. The family were passionately supportive of women's
rights. After Edith's mother died from tuberculosis in 1883, her father
married Jewish scientist and suffragette Hertha Marks in 1885. The
Ayrtons became acquainted with Anglo-Jewish writer Israel Zangwill
and in 1903, Edith and Zangwill were married. Edith and her half-
sister, Barbara Ayrton Gould, joined the Women's Social and Political
Union in 1907 together with Hertha, and all three women were
members of the Jewish League for Woman Suffrage (JLWS). Israel
Zangwill was an advocate for suffrage and was also a member of
the JLWS. During the years of their most intense campaigning, the
Zangwills had three children under 10 and Edith recorded in her diary
that the eldest would frequently run around the house shouting
"Votes for Women". Edith Zangwill was the author of six novels, one
of which, *The Call* (1924), was a suffrage novel with a central plot
about a woman scientist's experiences during the First World War and
clearly based on her stepmother.

"We were well aware that
this was a big show."
Robert Stanford Tuck

Photography credits

pp. 3, 10, 11, 15, 155 © Ian Lillicrapp/Jewish Museum London, p. 6 © Eyevine, pp. 8, 82, 220, 221 © Getty Images, pp. 13, 28, 34, 35, 90, 134, 140, 158, 162, 172, 182, 194, 205, 206, 210, 215, 218, 228, 230/231, 266, 278, pp. 14, 62, 95, 107, 120, 226, 240, 256 © Jewish Museum London, pp. 21, 22, 24, 33, 36, 59, 60, 74, 75, 78, 96, 101, 102, 104, 108, 110, 111, 118, 119, 123, 127, 146, 147, 157, 160, 167, 168, 169, 173, 174, 184, 188, 193, 199, 203, 212, 232, 236,247, 255, 267, 271 © under the Creative Commons (CC) licence, pp. 37, 40, 41 © Parliamentary Archive, pp. 38, 64, 65, 66, 69, 71, 76, 77, 79, 98, 100, 105, 106, 113, 114, 115, 124, 145, 150, 152, 161, 164, 165, 166, 170, 175, 197, 213, 214, 234, 237, 238, 239, 246, 253 © National Portrait Gallery, London, pp. 42, 67, 70, 73, 117, 178 © Family Image, pp. 43, 46, 47, 48, 52, 54, 56, 61, 92, 109, 125, 128, 148, 177, 201, 204, 207, 208, 254, 262, 265, 268 © Rex/Shutterstock, p. 45 © Bridgeman Images, pp. 51, 53 © New South Wales Art Gallery, p. 55 © Blitzwalkers, pp. 57, 58, 99, 103, 122, 143, 154, 176, 180, 196, 211, 222, 235, 257, 261, 263, 274 from the Public Domain, p. 63 © Photographers Direct, p. 68 © Newcastle Law School, p. 80 under the Creative Commons (CC) licence © Bryan Ledgard, p. 86 under the Creative Commons (CC) licence © Allan Warren, p. 91 © Science Photo Library, p. 97 © Jewish Chronicle, p. 112 © Pegasus Archive, pp. 116, 126, 153, 200, 202, 243, 244, 245, 248, 249, 250, 251, 252, 259, 263, 268, 274, 275, 276 © Topfoto, p. 121 © Jew Prom, p. 130 under the Creative Commons (CC) licence © Matt Buck, p. 139 under the Creative Commons (CC) licence © Jeffrey W. Bass, p. 142 © Andy Hall Photography, pp. 151, 217, 219, 269 © Webb & Webb Design Ltd., p. 156 © Ben Uri Gallery, P. 159 © Camera Press, p. 163 © John Harris/Report Digital, p. 171 © Royal Opera House, p. 181 © University of Nottingham, p. 198 © Miltary Archive, p. 209 © Mike Harding, p. 216 © IMW, p. 233 © Esther Salaman, p. 241 © Library of Congress, p. 242 © Ham and High, p. 260 © Sternians, p. 271, 272 © Wohl Foundation

Previous Squadron Leader Robert Stanford Tuck, in the cockpit of his Hawker Hurricane Mk I at Coltishall, January 1941